THE REAL

# Halloween

RITUAL AND MAGIC FOR KIDS AND ADULTS

THE REAL

# Halloween

RITUAL AND MAGIC FOR KIDS AND ADULTS

SHEENA MORGAN

BARRON'S

First edition for the United States, Canada, and Mexico
published by Barron's Educational Series, Inc., 2002.

First published in 2002 under the title The Real Halloween by Godsfield Press,
Laurel House, Station Approach, Alresford, Hants SO24 9JH, England

All inquiries should be addressed to:
Barron's Educational Series, Inc.
250 Wireless Boulevard
Hauppauge, New York 11788
http://www.barronseduc.com

International Standard Book No. 0-7641-2222-3

Library of Congress Catalog Card No. 2001097847

Printed and bound in China
9 8 7 6 5 4 3 2 1

The publishers would like to thank the following libraries for permission to reproduce copyright material:
BRIDGEMAN ART LIBRARY: pp: 56, Kunsthistorisches Museum, Vienna; 109, National Galleries of Scotland, Edinburgh; 117B, Wallace
Collection, London. CAMERON COLLECTION: pp: 12, 17, 19, 26, 27, 38. CORBIS: pp: 10–11, 13, 15, 18B, 21, 25, 29, 31, 35, 39, 40, 42, 43, 46,
54, 60–61, 68, 70, 71, 73, 104–105, 114, 120, 121. IMAGE BANK: pp: 6,7.

# CONTENTS

# THE REAL HALLOWEEN

*"Hey, hey for Halloween! Then the witches shall be seen,*

*Some in black and some in green, Hey, hey for Halloween!*

*Horse and hattock, horse and go, Horse and pellatis, Ho! Ho!"*

TRADITIONAL

LET'S NOT BEAT around the bush: Halloween is scary. It's a strange, unnatural night when goblins and ghouls, witches and werewolves, vampires and zombies roam freely through our streets in search of unsuspecting souls, ready to carry them off to the land of the fairy. October 31 is the date when we wait, quivering in anticipation, for the Witching Hour of midnight, when the spirits of the dead rise and walk the earth once more.

Halloween is also the only night of the year when we happily dress up as monsters and decorate our homes with skeletons and ghosts;

when we welcome guests with the sight of leering faces carved into Jack-o'-lanterns; and cheerfully send our children out into the night, to beg for candy from our neighbors, with the threat of a trick or a treat.

Our current festival evolved from a bewildering mix of ancient Celtic, Roman, and Anglo-Saxon rituals, incorporating both pagan and Christian traditions. In spite, or perhaps because of, its macabre nature and association with the dead, Halloween has endured as one of the most popular holidays on the calendar. This celebration has evolved into a unique event: a blending of the frivolous and the frightening, the secular, and the spiritual.

In the United States, more than anywhere, Halloween is big business, with millions of dollars spent every year on decorations and treats. In Mexico, Halloween is celebrated with gusto as Los Días de Los Muertos, The Days of the Dead. Families honor their ancestors by picnicking in cemeteries and decorating their relatives' graves with flowers and ribbons. Most of Catholic Europe still sees the festival of All Souls' Day (November 2) as a solemn religious observance, when the dead are remembered.

RIGHT *Pumpkins, carved into sinister faces, are traditional Halloween effigies.*

LEFT *Children love to dress up for Halloween.*

# ALL SAINTS' AND ALL SOULS'

THROUGHOUT EUROPE, *the festival days of All Saints' and All Souls' are widely celebrated by Catholics. While each country has its own traditions, the overall theme of these church services is sober contemplation and remembrance of the dead.*

IN MANY OF THE PREDOMINANTLY Catholic countries of Europe, such as Italy, Poland, Hungary, and Spain, November 1 has become a public holiday. In the southern German region of Bavaria and in Austria, Catholics celebrate the entire period between October 30 and November 8 as Seleenwoche, or All Souls' Week.

On All Saints' Day (November 1), most Catholics attend church services in honor of the saints, the martyrs, and those who have died for the Catholic faith. Many people also visit their local cemeteries to beautify the graves of their relatives with wreaths and small lanterns. Sometimes a special mass is said at the cemetery and the graves are sprinkled with holy water.

On November 2, or All Souls' Day, Catholics attend special Requiem masses, where they remember friends and family members who have died. Prayers for the dead are said and votive candles are lit in honor of their memory. Many Catholics also mark All Souls' Day by attending family gatherings or reunions where they renew friendships and remember their dead. All Saints' and All Souls' Day are so widely celebrated that many cities now provide dedicated bus, tram, and train services just to ferry people to and from churchyards over the two-day festival.

Neopagans in Europe, Australia, and North America honor their ancestors on October 31. They still use the ancient Celtic term Samhain, meaning "summer's end," to describe the night when the dead are traditionally believed to reappear. The Celts considered Samhain the most auspicious time for communicating with their dead. It was believed that on this night, any souls who had not yet passed into the paradise of the summer lands might return to wander the streets and visit their old homes once more.

Because the spirits of the other worlds were at large, the night of Samhain itself began

to be thought of as a supernatural time, when all forms of magic would naturally be more powerful. "Skrying," or fortune telling, casting spells, and making charms to ward off bad luck were all traditional Samhain pastimes.

Neopagans celebrate the festival today as a turning point between the old year and the new, and still see the night of October 31 as a gateway between the worlds. Many neopagans believe that, on the eve of Samhain, the veil separating the realms of the living and the dead is at its thinnest and that on this night, there is a better chance of being successful in communicating with their ancestors.

Wiccans accept death as an essential part of the natural cycle: they do not fear it, but instead see death as a gateway to another stage of existence. Many Wiccans celebrate Samhain with rites that are centered on the Celtic god of the Underworld, Cernunnos. These rites give the living an opportunity to recognize and to "feast" with death, and the dead an opportunity to make themselves known if that is their wish.

ABOVE *Many countries observe All Souls' Day with special prayers.*

LEFT *Tarot cards are often used by witches to foretell the future.*

When the rites are over, temples and magic circles are often left open for the dead to inhabit for the rest of the night. Offerings to the spirit world are made—food and wine are left out and a fire left burning.

In common with earlier peoples, neopagans also use the eve of Samhain as a favored time for divination. Skrying is still a common Samhain activity, with many modern witches using "Dark Mirrors" to look into the future. Some witches undertake pyromancy and search for messages from other realms in the flames of the Samhain bonfire. Some employ hydromancy while skrying in a cauldron filled with still water. Others prefer to use tarot cards or runes to try to foretell events at this magical turning point of the year.

# THE PAST

# THE CELTIC ORIGINS OF HALLOWEEN

ONE THOUSAND YEARS BEFORE *the beginning of the Christian era, the ancient Celts swept across central Europe to Britain. They brought with them their warrior culture, a passion for music and poetry, and, most importantly, the ability to create iron.*

LIKE MANY LATER INVADERS, the Celts drove Britain's indigenous inhabitants deep inland to the refuge of remote hills and forests. As a race, the Celts were notoriously warlike and quick to anger, and were greatly feared in battle by their foes. Plato, writing between c. 447–347 B.C.E., dismisses them as "drunken and combative," while 200 years later, Strabo calls them "war-mad and quick to fight."

There are several contemporary accounts of the horror that ferocious Celtic battle cries struck into the hearts of their enemies. "They are given to wild outbursts," the Roman historian Livy writes, "and fill the air with hideous song and varied shouts. Their battle songs, their yells and leapings, and the dreadful noise of arms as they beat their shields, are done to terrify their enemies."

Yet the Celts were great poets and lovers of music, art, jewelry, and rich displays of wealth. "They wear a striking kind of clothing," the philosopher Poseidonus (135–51 B.C.E) reports, "tunics stained in various colors, striped cloaks, ornaments of gold, torcs on their necks and bracelets on their arms and wrists. People of high rank wear dyed garments sprinkled with gold."

The Celts were undoubtedly cruel and implacable, yet they advocated learning and the healing arts. It was said they valued the poetry of their druid priests more highly than their chieftains' lives. This apparently contradictory behavior was a quintessential expression of the twin strands that ran through Celtic thought. For them, the balancing of opposites was of paramount importance.

LEFT *The Celts were notoriously belligerent, as this engraving illustrates.*

The Celtic calendar reflected their outlook on life. The year was divided into two distinct halves: summer and winter. Summer, from early May to the end of October, was the period of "the great sun," when light and the life force were at their strongest, and peace and plenty reigned. Winter, on the other hand, from November to the end of April, was the period of "the small sun" and signified darkness, death, and impending chaos.

## Fleadh nan Mairbh, the Feast of the Dead

Before the existence of calendars, the life of early herding and farming peoples was dictated by the phases of the moon and the changing seasons of the year. The end of the harvest marked the natural end of the year for the Celts, when plants died back and any available food was carefully preserved and stored. Samhain was the turning point between the end of summer and the beginning of the privations

ABOVE *To this day, Druid priests mark the winter and summer solstices.*

of winter. As the weather turned colder and the days grew shorter, the Celtic community would begin to prepare for the winter that lay ahead.

Samhain was also the period when cattle and sheep were brought down from the hills to their winter enclosures. Those animals that could not be kept through the winter were slaughtered, and communities once again began to rely on hunting for their meat. Throughout November, bonfires, or bone-fires, were lit all over Celtic Britain and the flames consumed and purified the butchered remains. November became known as the Black Month, or Blood Month.

Winter claimed many lives among the elderly and the very young. It is little wonder then, that "Fleadh nan Mairbh," the Feast of the Dead, evolved when slaughter was everywhere and the threat of starvation loomed over every community.

## Fire Rituals

As the land slipped into the gloom of winter, Samhain rituals evolved to protect struggling Celtic communities. Celts tried to appease their gods and the spirits of their ancestors with gifts, while blazing bonfires were used to drive back the powers of darkness.

For more than a thousand years, the bonfire, or tein, was central to Samhain rituals. Large bonfires were assembled in the center of every village and on top of every hill. The bonfire was built and a circular, sun-shaped trench dug around it. On the night of Samhain itself, all the fires in every village were extinguished. The central fire, or tein eigin, was lit and then each family took home a burning branch or ember to light their New Year's hearth fire from the blazing communal flame.

In Ireland, druid priests maintained a great bonfire, from which every village rekindled their own Samhain fires. The Tlachtga meath burned in the middle of the country on the sacred hill of hazel groves (Teamhair, or Tara).

BELOW *The stag, symbol of royalty and divinity, was often sacrificed at Samhain.*

At Samhain, the druids reviewed their laws and those who had transgressed were punished. The punishment for the most severe crimes (probably the infringement of religious taboos) was death on the flames of the Tlachtga meath. Eyewitnesses also described animals being sacrificed at this time. Horses were revered as magical creatures; wild boar were seen as symbols of courage and power; and the stag, set apart from all other animals by its high, branching antlers, represented both royalty and divinity.

Some think that the early Celts believed the souls of the recently deceased could not pass straight into the "summer lands." Instead they had to wait, lingering in woods and fields until Samhain, when the onset of winter drove them out of the countryside. The Celts believed that the dead not only needed the help of the living to find their way to the Underworld, but might even want to return to their old homes and families on the way.

While the Celts felt they had to appease the spirits of their ancestors, they were also pragmatic and did not want to encourage the dead to become too comfortable. Typically, Samhain fires served a dual purpose and the Celts saw no incongruity in using fire to both welcome and drive off wandering souls. Offerings of food and drink were left out, but empty hearths ensured that houses were cold and unwelcoming to visiting spirits. The central bonfire acted as a beacon, drawing the souls of the dead away from their previous homes. Hilltop bonfires were also lit, probably to guide spirits on their journey to the "summer lands," and village boundaries were delineated with flaming torches. These torches acted both to direct the souls onward and to prevent them from lingering too long.

RIGHT *Bonfires originated as a Samhain fire ritual to protect Celtic communities.*

# SPIRITS OF SAMHAIN

Cernunnos we call upon thee now,

Breast as white as milk, stag of seven tines

We call thee to us

Lip as red as blood, stag of seven tines

We call thee to us

Eye as black as night, stag of seven tines

We call thee to us

To guard us through the turning point of the year

THE CALL TO CERNUNNOS

## The Horned One

The ancient Celts worshipped various gods, and spirits of winter. Of these, Cernunnos, the Horned One, was of supreme importance. This horned figure, a fusion of both man and beast, is widely found in prehistoric cave art and symbolizes the enduring link between the hunter and the hunted.

Cernunnos represented the primal forces of life and death. His horns, symbols of divinity

16

and virility, showed his affinity with the stag and marked him as the sacrificial god of hunting, who both bestowed and took life. Cernunnos was often depicted with ram-headed serpents, with bags of coins, or holding precious metals. The serpents signaled esoteric knowledge, and the metal pointed to the fact that he was intimately linked with the earth and, by inference, with the Underworld. In time, one of Cernunnos' main aspects became that of the Lord of Death and Guardian of the Gateway to the Underworld.

Early Samhain rituals may have involved druid priests blackening their faces, wearing horns or masks, and performing shamanic dances to contact the gods of the Underworld. Certainly this practice still exists in many present cultures, where shamans don the costume of a spirit to become, or to commune with, that spirit.

In time, these ritual communications with the dead became debased: the descendants of the Celts still wore strange costumes and blackened their faces with soot, but this was done simply to scare away any evil spirits.

## Cailleach Bheur

In the Scottish highlands, the Cailleach Bheur, or Blue-Faced Hag, was known as the "daughter of the winter sun" and was the personification of winter. The Cailleach was reborn every Samhain eve and brought with her the cleansing snows of the coldest time of the year. Her totem animals were, like those of Cernunnos, the stag and the wolf.

The Cailleach crept over the land, killing any remaining crops with her magical staff and ensuring that nothing grew during the winter months. Her sovereignty lasted until Beltane (the eve of May 1), when the great sun of

ABOVE *The Blue-Faced Hag was the embodiment of winter.*

summer ousted the small sun of winter. Then the Cailleach threw away her magic staff and turned herself to stone to wait for winter.

Scottish farmers left the last sheaf of the harvest in the field and would not cut it before Samhain. It was known as the Auld Wife, the Carline, or the Cailleach and, when cut, was dressed as an old woman. Farmers took care to ensure the sheaf was cut before dusk, to prevent the Cailleach from becoming an evil witch. Her apron pockets were filled with bread and cheese and the Cailleach was carried in triumph back to the farm, where she presided over the Samhain feast. The Cailleach was usually kept in a place of honor until Beltane, when she was burned on the ritual fire. Today, decorative corn dolls are still made and displayed in rural, farming areas.

LEFT *Scottish farmers believed that the Cailleach Bheur brought with her cleansing snow.*

### Hwch ddu gwta

In North Wales, fear of Hwch ddu gwta, the Tailless Black Sow, held the countryside in terror each year on Samhain eve, or Nos Galan Gaeaf. Before dawn, large bonfires were lit along the hilltops and ridges, each village competing to keep its fire alight for the longest possible time. Apples were roasted in the embers and villagers would leap through the flames for good luck. As the flames began to die down, each inhabitant would throw a stone into the fire.

In a test of nerve, the locals would wait until the fire was almost out and the powers of darkness had begun to encroach on them once more. They would then race home shouting, "May the Tailless Black Sow take the hindmost!" The following morning, everyone would return to try to find his or her stones. Any missing or damaged stones meant bad luck or possible death for their owners.

BELOW *Monastery ruins on Great Skellig Island. Irish mythology abounds with superstition.*

ABOVE *The little people are notorious for playing mischievous tricks on humans.*

### The Little People

Samhain occurred at the pivotal point between the autumn equinox and the winter solstice and, as the Celts saw all turning points of the year as deeply magical, it assumed particular importance. It was seen as a spiritual gateway between the old and the new, the dead and the living, the spirit world and the natural world. In short, Samhain was seen as a powerful, magical doorway.

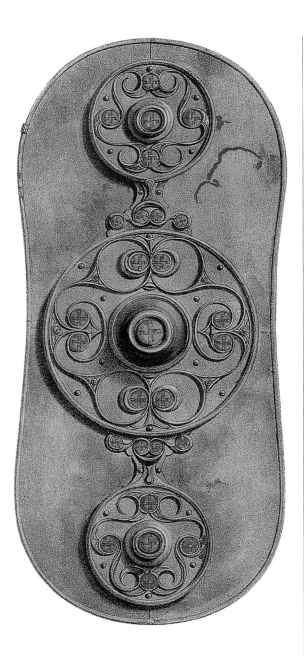

The Celts and their descendants believed that this doorway was open to all spirits and that the dead were not the only ones roaming free on Samhain eve. The Celts greatly feared the malicious interference of supernatural beings known as the puca, or little people. The puca were inhabitants of other worlds and were known to frequent holy wells and caves, but their favorite homes were barrows—the burial mounds of the Celtic dead.

These eerie creatures were usually distinguished by one particular characteristic, such as green skin, green or brown clothing, or a slightly smaller size. It was not until the Middle Ages that the puca began to be thought of as minute, winged creatures. Their features were always unusual and puca who were pretending to be human, for mischievous ends, usually could be identified by their unnaturally long noses or pointed ears.

The origin of "the little people" is unclear, although some scholars suggest that they were originally the revered souls of the long dead, which, over time, became degraded into tiny mischief-makers. Others put forward a compelling argument that the little people were the Brythons, aboriginal inhabitants of Britain, driven into hiding by the invading Celts.

The puca were renowned for "borrowing" from their human neighbors, often taking food, drink, fire, tools, and raw materials. It is easy to speculate how a defeated people, living in hiding and only venturing into villages to scavenge under cover of darkness, could have evolved into the magical puca. Traditional puca mischief—such as causing illness in cattle, souring milk, and spoiling crops, among other acts—might have been the work of hill-dwelling guerrilla bands bent on revenge.

### THE DAOINE SIDHE

Irish mythology describes the great Tuatha de Danann (the mythical god-like tribes of the goddess Dana), suffering a great change after their defeat by the Milesians. Those who remained in Ireland reportedly began dwelling underground and became known as the Daoine Sidhe, the people of the hills.

# THE CHRISTIAN ERA

WHEN CHRISTIANITY *was first introduced to Britain, pagans and Christians worshipped side by side. In fact, some pagans simply added Christ to their existing pantheon of gods. Many pagans originally saw Christianity as a new and effective type of magic—not something that would replace their ancient gods of hill, stream, and grove.*

## The Birth of Halloween

The populations of England, Scotland, Ireland, and Wales continued to practice their deep-rooted, ancient pagan rites well after the arrival of Christianity in the middle of the sixth century. Early Church fathers became increasingly concerned as the popularity of pagan festivals grew at the expense of Christian holy days.

BELOW *Gregory III linked the Christian All Saints' Day to the pagan Samhain.*

In 601 C.E., Pope Gregory I issued an edict to his missionaries about the beliefs and habits of the peoples he wanted to convert. Gregory realized that it would be impossible to obliterate native beliefs completely and so suggested to his priests that they "Christianize" them whenever possible.

If the indigenous people worshipped at a well, stone, or sacred grove, Gregory instructed his missionaries to consecrate them to Christ and let the worship continue. In seventh-century Ireland, sacred groves were so revered that a fine of three cows (hugely valuable at that time) was payable by anyone caught destroying the holy trees.

Samhain continued to be one of the most important and vigorously celebrated of the pagan festivals. In 609 C.E., Gregory's successor, Pope Boniface IV, declared May 13 All Saints' Day—a holy day on which to remember martyred saints and a suggested Christian alternative to the pagan Samhain. Unfortunately, while pagans were happy to add All Saints' Day to their calendar, they were unwilling to give up their existing festival of the dead and continued to celebrate Samhain with the same vigor as before.

By the eighth century, the Christian Church had adjusted many of its own principal holy

ABOVE *The lighting of church candles has ancient pagan origins.*

*Halloween Invocation to Bride (St. Brigid), to place her power:*

*Between us and the Fairy Hosts*
*Between us and the Hosts*
*of the Wind*
*Between us and*
*the Drowning Water*
*Between us and*
*the Heavy Temptations*
*Between us and the Shame*
*of the World*
*Between us and the*
*Death of Captivity.*

RELIGIOUS SONGS OF CONNAUGHT, VOL. II, 1920

days to coincide with existing pagan festivals. Christmas now fell at the end of December, when pagans already celebrated the winter solstice. Candlemas was tied to the fire festival of Bride (canonized as St. Brigid) and Annunciation Day, or Lady Day, was attached to the pagan celebration of the fertility goddess Oestara. The great solar festival that took place at the midsummer solstice was renamed St. John's Day, and Lughnasadh—the period of mourning for the Celtic sun god Lugh—became Loaf mass, or Lammas.

Intent on eradicating the ongoing power of pagan beliefs, Pope Gregory III (731–741 C.E.) followed in the footsteps of earlier Christian leaders and deliberately linked the Christian All Saints' Day to the pagan festival of Samhain. He moved All Saints' Day to November 1, where it gradually became known by the peasant population as All Hallows. Since Samhain traditionally fell on the night before All Hallows, it eventually became known as All Hallows' Even' or Hallowe'en.

While previous church leaders had tried to discourage Samhain traditions, such as the wearing of frightening costumes, Gregory III took a more practical approach and encouraged people to dress up in honor of the saints. Other traditions, such as begging for food or kindling, were legitimized by the Church, provided the food was for the poor, rather than to appease otherworld spirits.

The Church added a second day to the festival during the tenth century. All Souls' Day fell on November 2 and was dedicated to those souls still in purgatory. The souls of penitent sinners had to endure the temporary punishment of purgatory in order to be purified of venial sins. It was believed that lighting candles and saying prayers for the dead would shorten the length of time they were expected to suffer in purgatory before ascending to heaven.

# A Prayer for Long Life

I invoke the seven daughters of the sea who fashion the threads of long life
May three deaths be taken from me
May three periods of age be granted me
May seven waves of good fortune be dealt me
Phantoms shall not harm me in my journey
In my flashing course let without a hitch
My fame shall not perish. May old age come to me
Death shall not find me until I am old
I invoke the silver champion who has not died, who will not die
May a period be granted to me equal in worth to white bronze
May my double be destroyed. May my right be maintained
May my strength be increased. Let not my gravestone be raised
May death not meet me on my way
May my journey be secured
The headless adder shall not seize me
Nor the hard grey worm
Nor the headless black chafer
Neither shall they harm me
Nor a band of women
Nor a band of fairy hosts
Let increase of time be to me from the King of the Universe
I invoke Senach, of the seven priests of time

Who fairy women have reared on breasts of plenty

May my seven candles not be extinguished

1 am an indestructible stronghold

1 am an unshakeable rock

1 am a precious stone

May 1 live a hundred times a hundred years

Each hundred of them apart

1 summon to me their good gifts

May the grace of the Holy Spirit be upon me.

Domini est salus, Domini est salus, Domini est salus

Christi est salus, Christi est salus, Christi est salus

Super populum tuum, Domine, benedictio tua

*MISCELLANEA HIBERNIA, UNIV. ILLINOIS, VOL. II, 1916*

*Soul Day, Soul Day! We've been praying for the souls departed,*
*We pray good people give us a cake,*
*For we are all poor people well known to you before,*
*So give us a soul cake for charity's sake,*
*And your blessing we'll leave at your door. Soul! Soul for an apple or two,*
*If you have no apples, pears will do. If pears be scarce a cake from your pan*
*Give us some souling and we'll be gone*

TRADITIONAL

## Souling

Souling, or Soul Caking, soon became established as an acceptable Christian alternative to earlier pagan traditions of begging for food with which to appease the spirits. The custom was for children to go from door to door asking for money for the poor and a soul cake for themselves. For every cake given, they would say a prayer for the souls of the dead. As the children went from house to house, they shouted:

*A soul cake! A soul cake!*
*Have mercy on all Christian souls,*
*For a soul cake!*

John Aubrey's seventeenth-century account of a Souling day describes the cakes as being "about the bigness of 2-penny cakes," and notes, "n'ly all the visitors that day took one."

Soul cakes took many names and many forms: in Yorkshire, they were dark fruitcakes called Saumas (soul mass) cakes; in Scotland, they were known as Dirge Loaves and were flat, round buns of oat flour; in Northamptonshire, they were covered in caraway seeds and were fashioned into small buns.

Until the early twentieth century, Halloween was called Cake Day in the North of England. In what may have been a relic of earlier souling traditions, mothers baked small individual cakes for each of their children. It was essential that each cake was a different flavor.

Although altered over the years, the custom of Souling survived in Staffordshire and Cheshire until the early twentieth century and

ABOVE *Soul caking still survives in some parts of England.*

has since grown in popularity. In Great Budworth, groups of children still go from door to door soul caking. This entails the performance of a verse and chorus of a traditional souling song, for which they receive a small cash reward.

The Antrobus, Comberbatch, and Great Budworth Soul Cakers still perform their traditional mummers' plays and Morris dances, around All Souls' Day. Part of the Soul Cakers' performance involves the entrance of the Wild Horse, which leaps around the crowd, snapping his jaws. The head of the horse is actually a painted horse's skull, wired together so that the teeth can snap shut. The use of a real skull may mark the performance as one of genuine antiquity and may link Christian Soul Caking with earlier pagan rites. Horses were considered one of the most magical of animals by the Celts and would have been paraded around the village before being sacrificed on the Samhain fires.

ABOVE *Morris dances are performed around All Souls' Day.*

This night we come a souling,
good nature to find,
And we hope you'll remember
it's Soul Caking time!
Christmas is coming and
the geese are getting fat,
Please put a penny in
the Old Man's hat.
If you haven't got a penny
a ha'penny will do,
If you haven't got a ha'penny,
God bless you!

TRADITIONAL

## The Reformation

During the Reformation and Counter-Reformation of the Church, Halloween was outlawed and re-established on numerous occasions. Such was the irrepressible popularity of the festival, however, that it survived, re-named and reinterpreted as Bonfire Night.

By 1517, the festival of All Hallows' Eve had become a popular and raucous event. Martin Luther published his criticisms of the Roman Catholic Church on October 31 in an attempt to draw attention to what he considered the abuses of the Church. Luther's protest was to have a profound effect on

ABOVE *Under Elizabeth I, the celebration of Halloween was no longer permitted in England.*

RIGHT *Superstitious belief in wicked fairies and spirits persisted.*

Christianity worldwide. It led to the Protestant Reformation causing bitter enmity between Catholics and Protestants. Eventually leading to the rupture of the Christian Church into numerous competing factions, to the dissolution of the monasteries in England, and, ultimately, to war.

At the end of the sixteenth century, religious practice in England had gone through a series of seismic changes and Halloween had been banned and reinstated several times. Henry VIII dissolved the Catholic monasteries and declared himself head of the Protestant Church of England in 1534. His son, Edward VI, went on to introduce Protestant services in English churches during his reign. The celebration of Halloween was prohibited throughout the land.

### Elizabeth I

Just six years after Edward's accession to the throne he was dead, and Mary I ("Bloody Mary"), a loyal Catholic, immediately undertook the restoration of the Roman Catholic bishops to England. England returned to Roman Catholicism once more, and Halloween returned to the calendar.

When Mary died from cancer in 1558, her successor, Elizabeth I, repealed all previous Catholic legislation. Having already witnessed her father's destruction of the Catholic monasteries and his self-appointment as figurehead of the Church of England, Elizabeth continued to oppose the Catholic Church. She firmly believed that a Protestant

England with herself as ruler of the Church as well as State would prove stronger both socially and politically. In 1586, in a bid to consolidate the Protestant future of England, a strict system of religious rules was enforced, making attendance at Protestant churches compulsory. Catholics continued to worship, but in secret, hiding their priests in concealed rooms or "priest holes." Anyone caught harboring a priest was subject to the harshest punishment.

Elizabeth executed Mary Stuart, Queen of Scots, her most dangerous Catholic rival. Now re-established, the Protestant Church once again denied the existence of saints and so, during the Reformation, all celebrations involving the saints were forbidden. Halloween no longer officially existed.

Despite the strict religious dictums of the Church, a widespread belief in otherworldly and supernatural spirits remained strong and could not be suppressed. Superstition thrived and continued to persist. For example, during the seventeenth century a Register of Deaths records three people being "frightened to death by fairies" and one man being "led into a horse pond and drowned by a Will o' the Wisp."

The pagan vitality of Halloween could not be easily extinguished, and the bonfires and revelry of the festival soon found another outlet, attaching themselves to November 5, Bonfire Night.

### THE GREGORIAN CALENDAR

While the Church was going through a spectacular upheaval, so was the calendar. In 1582, Pope Gregory XIII altered the way in which each year was calculated. He abandoned the earlier Julian calendar of the Romans and established a year of 365 days, with a leap year every four years. The new Gregorian calendar meant that all of the feast days moved slightly.

## Guy Fawkes

*Rumour, rumour, pump and derry*
*Prick his heart and burn his body*
*And send his soul to purgatory*

Elizabeth's heir, the Protestant James I, had been King of England for just over two years when an attempt was made on his life by a small band of Catholic zealots. On November 5, 1605, Guy Fawkes and his companions tried to restore the

*Remember, Remember*
*the fifth of November,*
*Gunpowder, treason, and plot,*
*I see no reason*
*why gunpowder treason,*
*Should ever be forgot.*

*Guy Fawkes, Guy Fawkes,*
*he's intent,*
*To blow up the Houses*
*of Parliament,*
*Three score barrels of powder below,*
*Poor old England to overthrow.*

*By God's providence he was catched,*
*With a black lantern and*
*a burning match.*
*Hollar, Hollar boys,*
*ring the bells ring!*
*Hollar, Hollar boys,*
*God save the King!*

Catholic faith by blowing up the King and the members of both Houses of Parliament. The affair became known as the "Gunpowder Plot" when two tons of gunpowder were found hidden in the cellars of Parliament.

The following year, at the King's instigation, Bonfire Night was established in England. An Act of Parliament was passed, setting aside a night of "publique thanksgiving to Almightie God, everie yeere on the fifte day of November." Ostensibly, the night was meant to commemorate the death of a traitor and the rescue of the King. In reality, the population saw Bonfire Night as replacing and fulfilling the role of outlawed Halloween. They ignored the official reason and seized the opportunity to celebrate November 5 exactly as they had earlier celebrated Halloween, by begging for kindling, lighting large fires, parading through the streets, and dressing up in various frightening costumes.

## Bonfire Boys

*Guy! Guy! Poke him in the eye!*
*Put him on the fire top and*
*there let him die*

With the establishment of Bonfire Night, James I also introduced the Scottish tradition of burning an effigy of a witch. He encouraged the first Bonfire Night revelers to burn models of Guy Fawkes, in memory of the traitor's capture and execution.

Nowhere was this new tradition more warmly embraced than in the small town of Lewes, on the south coast of England. The largely Protestant community there had suffered under the reign of the Catholic Mary I and had seen 17 townspeople burned as heretics in 1557. Protestant fervor ran high.

Our king's a valiant soldier
With his blunderbuss on his shoulder
Cocks his pistol, draws his rapier,
Pray give us something for his sake,
here!
A stick, a stake for
our good king's sake
If you won't give one, I'll take two
The better for me,
the worse for you!

TRADITIONAL

Bonfire Night celebrations in Lewes revolved around a central, loudly-voiced theme painted on banners and placards: "No Popery." By the seventeenth century, elaborate torch-lit parades were being organized to mark the night. These events were marshalled by rowdy groups of young men, known as "The Bonfire Boys."

In 1679, a contemporary magazine, *The Domestick Intelligence*, described a typical Bonfire Night at Lewes complete with a fake Pope and a masked Guy Fawkes. "This day was celebrated with extraordinary solemnity, there being a long procession, not unworthy of note. Just before 'the Pope' marched Guy Faux with his 'dark lanthorn,' being booted and spurred after the old fashion and wearing a vizard with a long nose."

*We want a twig,*
*to make it alight*
*Hatchets and duckets,*
*beetles and wedges*
*If you don't give us some,*
*we'll pull down your hedges*

TRADITIONAL: HEADINGTON, OXON

LEFT *The Protestant memorial in Lewes, East Sussex, England.*

These festivities came to a climax with the burning of an effigy of the Pope. The tradition exists to this day in Lewes but there is now no ill feeling between Catholics and Protestants.

Such was the devotion to established bonfire sites that fires continued to be lit on their traditional Samhain locations. As towns had expanded, however, these sites, once safely in open fields, were now enveloped by houses and shops. Huge fires, some 20 feet (7 meters) in height, were lit in the middle of the main street, putting the lives of local residents at risk. It was not until the early twentieth century, with the widespread introduction of flammable tarmac road surfaces, that bonfires began to be sited at a safe distance from houses.

Over the years, the south coast of England became infamous for Bonfire Night

### A PENNY FOR THE GUY

Today, English children still make scarecrowlike figures from old clothes and straw. They sit, begging, at street corners for "a penny for the Guy." Any money collected is usually spent on fireworks or candies.

disorderliness. Twenty-eight teams of Bonfire Boys competed to put on the best show and participants in the various torch-lit parades ran into the hundreds.

Boisterous mischief-making developed into full-scale rioting during the eighteenth and nineteenth centuries. In Oxford, street fighting between Gowns (students) and Towns (the local population) came to a head at Halloween, when serious assaults and beatings were routine. Contemporary accounts from the south coast of England describe "firing guns and pistols, kicking burning tar barrels over in the streets, attacking constables and breaking windows," as commonplace Halloween events. On one occasion, a policeman was killed

ABOVE *Bonfire night revelers in Lewes dressed as bishops, bearing burning crosses.*

during an affray. When, in an attempt to calm the Bonfire Night unrest, a local council tried to ban the procession, death threats were made against the council members. These were taken seriously and Bonfire Night was rapidly reinstated.

By 1647, the English Parliament had passed a law abolishing Christmas, but Bonfire Night survived. The fact that Bonfire Night is still celebrated yearly, in addition to Halloween, is indicative of the importance that this time of year and this form of celebration still hold for the English.

31

# HALLOWEEN IN BRITAIN

*"Halloween, a night 'o' tein. A can'le in a custock*
*A howkitt neep wi' glowerin' e'en. Tae flaig bathe witch and warlock."*
*(Halloween, a night of fire, A candle in a kale stalk. A hollowed*
*turnip, with glowering eyes. To fright both witch and warlock.)*

GUISERS' SONG

By THE NINETEENTH CENTURY, polite society had transformed Halloween into nothing more than an occasion for decorous parties. In an age of industrial expansion and technological development, the rapidly growing middle class refused to admit belief in anything that was not forward-thinking. Genteel Victorians disapproved of unruly Halloween mischief-making: instead they encouraged nothing more sinister than demure parlor games based on romantic divination.

Young ladies still wanted to find out who their future husbands would be and so participated in sedate activities such as "The Apple at the Glass." Girls would eat an apple at midnight, while combing their hair in front of a mirror. Any reflection was supposed to show their future spouse.

Apple seeds were placed on girls' cheeks in order to tell which of two potential suitors would be the more faithful. Each seed was named after a young man and a rhyme was recited: "Pippin, pippin stick thee there, Who is true thou mayest declare." The seed adhering to the cheek for the longest represented the most faithful suitor.

While the town-dwelling middle classes rejected the more supernatural elements of Halloween, country people clung doggedly to their traditional beliefs. Areas such as the Highlands of Scotland, the North of England, Ireland, and Wales kept alive the old customs of October 31, which may have retained elements of ancient Samhain traditions.

Among the descendants of the Celts, lighting bonfires was still central to every Halloween celebration. Superstition remained

ABOVE *Apple seeds would determine the more faithful of two suitors.*

32

ABOVE *A future spouse might appear in the mirror at midnight.*

strong and, in the aftermath of the witch-hunts of previous centuries, witches were believed to take to the air on broomsticks to harass the population every Halloween.

In Lancashire, until the late nineteenth century, Halloween was called "Tan Day" from the Celtic tein, or fire, and pitchforks full of burning hay were flung into the air to scare witches. The heat and smoke of the central, communal bonfire was also thought to drive away any airborne witches.

Scottish superstitions ran deeper and darker than most. In memory of the fact that Scotland had been the only country in Britain to burn to death its supposed witches, children in Aberdeenshire would run around their villages, banging on doors and shouting: "Gae's a peat tae burn the witch!" This practice continued until the early twentieth century.

Effigies of witches were commonly burned on the Halloween bonfire; a tradition that merged into that of burning Guy Fawkes on November 5. Queen Victoria herself recalled seeing one such burning at the end of the nineteenth century, while at Balmoral Castle. A dummy of an old woman called the Shandy Dan was wheeled in a cart to the center of a large gathering of villagers and then tossed onto the fire with much celebration.

## Punkie Night

In the village of Hinton St. George, in Somerset, residents celebrate Punkie Night in addition to Halloween. The festival is named after the lanterns, or punkies, which adults and children still carry around town on the last Thursday in October. The tradition began on All Hallows' Eve in 1840 when the men of the village were particularly late in returning from the fields. Worried that evil spirits, or witches, could have harmed them, the women set out in search of their husbands. As they walked they fashioned lanterns out of the turnips and mangold wurzels (a type of beet) that were growing in the fields and carried these "punkies" above their heads to light their way.

*It's Punkie night tonight*
*Give us a candle, give us a light*
*If you don't you'll get a fright*

*It's Punkie night tonight*
*Adam and Eve would never believe*
*It's Punkie night tonight.*

## Leeting the Witches

Within living memory, Leeting, or Lighting the Witches, took place every Halloween in Pendle, Lancashire. Between 11 p.m. and midnight, courageous townsfolk would assemble at the Malkin Tower to perform the ceremony. The tower was the one-time home of the famous Pendle Witch, Old Mother Demdike, and local people still believed the area to be imbued with supernatural power. The bravest of those in the gathering would carefully carry a lighted candle clockwise around the tower. If the flame stayed steady, it was believed any malevolent powers would vanish. If the flame flickered, or worse, blew out, bad luck or death would soon follow.

## Turning the Devil's Stone

This tradition still takes place in Shebbear, Devon, on November 5. Just after dark, a procession sets off from The Devil's Stone pub and makes its way through the village. This march is usually led by the local vicar and made up of villagers and well-wishers. The Stone itself weighs more than a ton and lies in the middle of town, on the green next to the church. At the stroke of midnight, the church bells ring out and the stone is turned over with long iron bars. Residents of Shebbear believe that turning the stone ensures good luck and the fertility of crops and cattle in the following year. Any failure to turn the stone would result in ill luck befalling the village.

## Hallan Day or Allan Day

In St. Ives in Cornwall, Halloween was celebrated as Allan Day until the late nineteenth century. Large apples known as fairy apples were sold in special markets and were given as love tokens, or gifts, to bring good luck. Recipients of these Allan Apples put them under their pillows in order to dream of future lovers. It was thought that eating the apple early in the morning would make any prophetic dreams come true.

## Saining the Fields

It was common for farming communities to spread any remaining ashes from the Halloween bonfire over their fields to "sain," or purify, them. Halloween ashes were thought to be particularly effective both for cleansing the land and ensuring its fertility. A persistent example of saining the fields was to be found in Poulton-le-Fylde in Lancashire until the late nineteenth century. Part of the village was known as Purgatory

ABOVE *The tar-barrel tradition survives in Devon, southwest England, to this day.*

Field and villagers believed that saining these areas would actually help the souls of the dead to pass through purgatory more quickly. Every Halloween and All Souls' Day, bonfires were lit and, in addition to the ashes, flaming pitchforks of hay were tossed over the soil.

## Tar-Barrel Running

A visit to Ottery St. Mary in Devon on November 5 is not for the faint-hearted, as the men and boys of the village still carry on the ancient Samhain tradition of "tar-barrel running." Teams of boys, watched closely by officials, start off the celebrations in the

ABOVE *The tar-barrel tradition survives in Devon, southwest England, to this day.*

afternoon. They set light to small tubs filled with tar and roll them around the village streets. As the evening progresses the men's teams join in with much larger casks of tar.

The tar barrels are set alight and flames pour out at either end, creating "horns" of fire. As the barrels careen wildly through the streets, watching crowds often have to leap out of their way to safety. The dramatic evening culminates with a fair and the lighting of a huge bonfire in the middle of the village square.

## The Highlands and Islands

In the Western Isles, it remained common for food to be left out for ancestral spirits. As recently as the 1850s, Highland crofters made offerings in the fields with these words:

*This I give to thee, Oh Fox, spare my lambs*
*This I give to thee, Oh Hooded Crow, spare my lambs*
*This I give to thee, Oh Eagle, spare my lambs*

They believed that the souls of the dead inhabited these predators and might exact revenge if not pacified with gifts.

Until the middle of the nineteenth century, communities on the Scottish island of Lewis continued to make Halloween sacrifices to the sea-god, Shoney. On Halloween night, a man was chosen to wade into the waves and offer a libation of ale to the sea, saying: "Shoney, I give you this cup of ale, hoping that you will be so kind to give us lots of sea-ware for enriching the ground this ensuing year."

The villagers went to their church for a short ceremony, then carried a vat of beer to their fields, where they spent the night drinking, singing, and dancing.

If Scottish farmers had to make a journey on Halloween night, they carried sprigs of rowan to ward off any malicious witchcraft. So widespread was the belief in the efficacy of rowan that it was often used in walking sticks and riding crops. A popular saying of the time claimed:

BELOW *The Scottish Highlands, where the belief in ancestral spirits was widespread.*

"If your whip stock's made of Rowan,
You can ride through any town."

Halloween was known as Mischief Night, and in Scotland hordes of youths wearing masks called Halfins took the notion of mischief to its limits. Turfs were placed over chimneys to smoke residents out of their homes, turnips and carrots were hurled against windows, ploughs were moved to neighboring farms, and gangs rampaged through villages, trying to wreck as many of their neighbors' bonfires as they could. An account of Halloween night in 1835 describes 30 bonfires in a single ten-mile stretch of countryside.

## Guisers

By the nineteenth century, the old Samhain tradition of disguising oneself to fool evil spirits had become formalized into "guising" in Scotland. Troops of children and older boys still wore outlandish costumes, blackened their faces, and went from door to door, but instead of simply begging for food or money, they began to perform songs, music, and poems. Rowdy groups would bang loudly on windows and doors, demanding entrance to give their performance and collect their reward. They usually warned homeowners of their presence by singing songs as they roamed the town.

In Ireland, guisers were just as unruly. Teams of boys wearing antlered masks would run from farm to farm, whooping and blowing horns as loudly as possible. They would hammer on the farmer's door, proceed to chant a traditional verse in Gaelic, and then demand money or "builin," a specially-prepared bread.

The night's Halloween and
the morn's Hallow day
Gin ye want a true love
it's time ye were away
Tally on the window board
Tally on the Green
Tally on the window board,
the night's Halloween.

Anocht Oidhche Shamna,
a Mhongo Mango.
Sop is na fuinneogaibh,
dúnta na dúirse,
Eirigh id' shuidhe,
a bhean an tighe,
Eirigih siar go banamháil,
tar aniar go flaitheamháil,
Tabhair leat ceapaire aráin agus
ime ar dhath do leacain fhéin;
A mbeidh léim ghirrfiagh dhe
aoirde ann agus coiscéim choiligh
dhe im air.

Oh, Mongo Mango, Halloween tonight
Straw up the windows
and close the doors
Rise up housewife,
go inside womanly,
return hospitably,
Bring with you a slice of bread,
and butter as red as your cheek
As high as a hare's jump with a
cock's step of butter on it!

*AN CLAID HEAMH SOLUIS, 1960*

# HALLOWEEN IN AMERICA

*"In the name of God, Amen. We, whose names are underwritten, the Loyal Subjects of our dread Sovereign Lord, King James, by the Grace of God King, Defender of the Faith. Having undertaken for the Glory of God, and Advancement of the Christian Faith, and the Honour of our King and Country, a voyage to plant the first colony in the northern parts of Virginia."*

THE MAYFLOWER COMPACT, 1620

## The Pilgrim Fathers

Despite being the son of the zealously Catholic Mary Queen of Scots, James I of England was unquestionably a Protestant King. At the same time, he strongly disapproved of the wave of new Protestant sects that were evolving at the end of the sixteenth century. In particular, James resented Puritanism, which he saw as

the "upstart" behavior of a group of separatists who insisted their first allegiance was to God and not to the King.

During James' reign, Cambridge University became a center of Puritan philosophy and some of the students there eventually founded a Puritan church. Other Puritan groups were forming at the same time. One such was based in Nottinghamshire and was led by William Brewster and the Rev. Richard Clifton. Local animosity toward the Nottinghamshire Puritans was so great that they left England for Holland in the early 1600s. Some later returned in 1619 to join with another group of English Puritans intent on traveling, as "pilgrims," to the New World.

The Pilgrim Fathers set sail in the *Mayflower* for Plymouth, Massachusetts, in 1620. In the creation of this new Puritan church, Christmas, Easter, and all Catholic saints' days,

LEFT *The Pilgrim Fathers sailed to the New World in the* Mayflower.

including Halloween, were unconditionally rejected. The Puritans believed that festivals were merely the inventions of humankind and should be abandoned. So strict was their code that church attendance was required by law. At one point, the celebration of Christmas was an offense. The Puritans celebrated only three types of religious holiday—the Sabbath, "Days of Praise and Thanksgiving," and "Days of Fasting and Humiliation."

Halloween disappeared from the calendar for a period in America, but its main elements—the traditional celebration of the harvest and opportunities for merry-making—became attached, over time, to the custom of Thanksgiving. This date was eventually fixed as the last Thursday of November.

## Thanksgiving

"Our harvest being gotten in, our governor sent four men on fowling, so that we might after a special manner rejoice together after we had gathered the fruit of our labours. Many of the Indians coming amongst us, and among the rest their greatest King Massasoit, with some ninety men, whom for three days we

ABOVE *The celebration of Thanksgiving originated with the Puritan settlers.*

entertained and feasted." Edward Winslow, *Mourt's Relation* (1621).

The original Puritan settlers almost starved during their first year in America and were saved only by the intervention of the indigenous population. The Algonquin tribes already held a thanksgiving festival in early winter, at the end of their growing year and it was natural that the Puritans should link their Thanksgiving festival to this. By the middle of the seventeenth century, Thanksgiving was an established celebration in the eastern colonies and, in 1777, Continental Congress declared the first nationwide American Thanksgiving.

While Halloween had been completely rejected, settlers in Massachusetts were less inclined to give up Bonfire Night, which remained an extremely well-attended event.

In Salem, which became notorious for its witch hunts, local judge Samuel Sewell recorded a typical Bonfire night in 1685. "Friday night being fair," he wrote, "about 200 hallow'd about a fire on the common."

## Bonfire Night in Nineteenth-Century America

By the 1780s, Bonfire Night had grown enormously popular all across America. A contemporary description mentions "punch, wine, bread and cheese, apples, and bonfires this evening at Salem, and a swarm of tumultuous people attending." It is significant that the eyewitness lists everything that was once considered necessary for a pagan celebration of Samhain—food and drink, a bonfire, and apples, a food that has always had strong associations with the underworld.

## Harvest Parties

As settlers began to spread out across America in the early nineteenth century, farming communities began to meet at harvest time, in

ABOVE *Traditional turnip lanterns were reinvented using pumpkins.*

LEFT *Halloween quickly became popular in America.*

addition to their Thanksgiving celebrations. Communities shared the typical tasks associated with the end of the growing season: corn and grain were dried, and meat was salted for winter; barns were raised; women met for quilting bees; and children held taffy pulls and made candy apples.

These harvest work-parties eventually evolved into more traditional parties with storytelling, music, and square dancing.

40

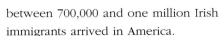

Party-goers began to revive earlier Halloween traditions, such as telling ghostly tales and trying to discover what the future had in store. Classic Halloween games, involving apples and nuts, were played in order to discover the identity of future spouses.

## The Reintroduction of All Hallows' Day

While immigrants from the Scottish highlands brought with them some of the ancient traces of Samhain in their Halloween celebrations, it was the huge influx of Irish Catholic immigrants, in the mid-nineteenth century, that brought about the real revival of Halloween. After the Irish potato famine of 1845–49,

between 700,000 and one million Irish immigrants arrived in America.

While the religious observed All Hallows' Day on November 1, most of the immigrant population preferred the fun of Halloween night. Traditional turnip lanterns—punkies or tumpshies—were reinvented using pumpkins, which were much more readily available. The newly arrived, near-starving immigrants also quickly revived the ancient traditions of guising, mischief-making, and, most importantly, begging for food door to door.

By the end of the American Civil War in 1865, the eve of All Hallows was widely celebrated by Catholics and Scottish Episcopalians, but it was still not at this point a national celebration. It took the power of the press to generate nationwide interest. The earliest articles promoting Halloween were aimed at mothers, encouraging them to celebrate the holiday on behalf of their children. One of the first appeared in *Godey's Lady's Book*, an influential women's magazine, in 1872. Quarterly reviews and newspapers followed suit, and Halloween rapidly became one of the most popular and widely enjoyed Victorian holidays, celebrated with fancy dress parties and bonfires.

Halloween also retained its earlier association with romantic fortune-telling. Unmarried youngsters began to treat Halloween gatherings as matchmaking events. Parties invariably included kissing games and mistletoe was frequently hung up at Halloween to encourage youngsters to kiss. Guests also took part in apple and nut divinations to discover details of future romances. One such game was known as "The Walnut Fortune." Before the party, the host carefully opened a quantity of walnuts and replaced the kernels with slips of paper bearing romantic fortunes, which would pair off single guests. Each guest would choose a fortune and then read it aloud.

41

## Recent Halloween Traditions

Recent Halloween celebrations have shown history repeating itself. From the demure parlor games of the Victorians, Halloween began to reassert itself as a night of unlicensed rowdiness. These pranks escalated in seriousness until the middle of the twentieth century, when civic leaders grew concerned over the safety of their citizens. It was only the outbreak of World War II that put an end to excessive Halloween practical jokes.

The success of a schoolchildren's Halloween parade in Allentown, Pennsylvania, prompted the town of Anoka, Minnesota, to

ABOVE *Children wear costume and go out trick-or-treating on Halloween night.*

hold the first official civic celebration of Halloween in 1921. The event involved costume parades and bonfires and also saw the introduction of "trick-or-treating" for children.

With the return of guising in its new "trick-or-treat" form, Halloween's reputation as a night for pranks and misbehavior was re-established. While younger children simply asked for candies with the threat of a trick, older children were determined to carry through elaborate practical jokes.

RIGHT *The rituals of Halloween remain as popular as ever, particularly for children.*

Mischief-making began to reach the same boisterous level as in Ireland, Scotland, and the North of England. In country towns, carts and farm equipment were dismantled and moved and outside toilets overturned. Favored pranks for city dwellers included, among other things, stealing garbage cans and stacking them in the middle of an intersection, or rubbing soap on trolley car tracks, causing the wheels to spin around uselessly.

Such was the enthusiasm for pranks and misbehavior that civic authorities began to fear that Halloween tricks had simply become vandalism. In 1939, in Chicago alone, more than one thousand windows were broken on Halloween night. All this stopped with the outbreak of World War II, when playing Halloween tricks was condemned as being "against the war effort" and thus vehemently discouraged.

In 1950, Halloween trick-or-treating took on a much worthier tone when a group of Philadelphia teenagers collected money instead of candies and donated their collection to UNICEF (United Nations International Children's Emergency Fund). The idea was taken up across the continent and collecting for UNICEF has become a widely established Halloween tradition.

Halloween has always been a night of misrule and the outrageous. In recent years, it has been adopted by the gay community in America as an opportunity for extravagant costume parades. The annual Greenwich Village parade in New York City began in the early 1970s and has grown in popularity ever since. The city now hosts a seven-day Halloweek festival. This tradition has been taken up across the country, with events taking place in San Francisco, New Orleans, and Key West.

Herein are collated ideas for the Halloween hostess which we believe will be instrumental in making a jolly and characteristic Witch Night party. Two points have been kept in mind... to give practical suggestions that can be carried out easily with little labor and expense and to offer fresh material which will be unusual as well as appropriate.

DENNISON'S *BOGEY BOOK*, 1912

# The Days of the Dead

The Mexican festival of The Days of the Dead is unique: a joyful celebration of life and a remembrance of those who have died. The Days of the Dead are celebrated all over Mexico and have evolved from a combination of ancient Aztec and modern Catholic traditions. In the United States, Mexican and Latino communities are beginning to observe The Days of the Dead as an addition to Halloween.

The original, pre-conquest festival took place at the end of August and coincided with the migration of Monarch butterflies—believed by the Aztecs to be departed souls returning to their homes. The Aztecs therefore dedicated the month of Miccailhuitontli to the Dead. During the festivities, offerings of candies were made to Mictecacihuati, the Goddess of Death. After the Spanish conquest, the date of the festival was forcibly moved to November 1 and 2. As earlier Christian church fathers had done, the invading Catholics annexed a pagan event by tying it to a Christian holiday. Like its European counterpart Halloween, The Days of the Dead incorporated indigenous pagan celebration and ritual, but also introduced Christian observance.

For weeks in advance, stores stock ingredients for the celebration: multi-colored wreaths, "papel picado" (intricately decorated tissue), and brightly-colored votive candles. Bakers and confectioners display huge piles of sugar skulls, coffins, and "pan de muerto"— bread shaped like the bones of the dead. Some also sell macabre little human figures, made of brown bread, known as "animas" (souls).

Families go to great lengths to create a beautiful altar, or "offrenda de muertos." The altar usually has three tiers, each covered in colored tissue; white is the favorite choice because it means hope, but many altars are

44

covered in purple tissue, which symbolizes the pain of separation. Photographs of the dead are placed on the top tier, with candles representing the four points of the compass. On the second level, three sugar skulls represent the Holy Trinity, and on the lowest tier, a large central skull symbolizes the ultimate Giver of Life.

Once the key elements are in place, the altar is decorated with more candles, bunches of marigolds, piles of candies, pan de muerto, and fruit. If the dead enjoyed drinking or smoking, packets of cigarettes and bottles of tequila are added to the altar so the dead can take pleasure in these when they revisit their homes. It is common to leave out soap, water, and a towel, so the dead can wash after their journey back from the grave.

In the streets, coffins containing living people disguised as corpses are carried around and the crowds, dressed in skeleton, mummy, and ghost costumes, throw candies and flowers into the open caskets. Parks are decorated with Calaca models of "Las Cavaleras" (skeletons), and these figures are shown enjoying life beyond the grave.

On the evening of November 1, families remember any children who have died, known as "angelitos," or little angels. On November 2, families honor the adult dead by visiting their local cemeteries. During the day, graves are tidied and decorated. Families then spend the whole of the night at the graveside, picnicking, singing, and playing music in remembrance of their dead. Until recently, it was customary for Mexican families to store the bones of their relatives in a tomb. The tombs were opened and the bones displayed during "Los Dias de las Muertos" before being sealed up again for the next 12 months.

# FAIRIES, WITCHES, AND MONSTERS

HALLOWEEN PROVIDES *a unique opportunity to embrace the things that frighten us the most and, by confronting them, to lessen their power over us.*

## Symbols of Halloween

Ancient peoples were terrified by the spirits of their dead ancestors, a fear that no longer preoccupies most modern societies. However, as we have become more sophisticated and more knowing, we have introduced new and increasingly more frightening elements to the traditions of Halloween.

In the early Middle Ages, the Christian Church fostered a profound distrust of women and, in particular, of female sexuality, which was considered to be a corrupting influence. These widespread fears contributed to the witch-hunting crazes that spread across Europe. While both men and women were accused of

BELOW *Dorothy and the witch, from the 1939 film,* The Wizard of Oz.

witchcraft, most people thought of witches as malicious women who, having made a pact with the devil, worked magic at night to allow them to fly, to change shape, and to control the weather. It is no surprise, then, that witches became associated with the night of Halloween and have remained one of its most enduring symbols through the years.

Ancient myths of the little people—supernatural creatures that could help or hinder—also became linked to October 31 during the Middle Ages. On Halloween it was believed that the most malevolent of these fairies, goblins, and imps were active. People actually feared that they could be spirited away by fairies if they were foolish enough either to forget their annual offering of food or to venture outside without a suitable disguise.

By the eighteenth century, a new horror, the vampire, had entered the British catalog of monsters. While vampire myths date back at least a thousand years and occur all over the world, little was known of them in Britain until a series of highly-publicized Serbian vampire trials, which took place between 1721 and 1734. Most of the trial accounts shared the same basic elements: the return of the vampire from the dead, its preying on human flesh at night, and the drinking of human and animal blood. The publication of the Gothic horror

novel *Dracula*, fixed the image of the depraved vampire in the public imagination forever.

For hundreds of years, people also believed that werewolves metamorphosed from man to wolf during the period of the full moon and preyed on humans. Their association with the moon linked them with the night of Halloween. Add to that their predilections— rape, murder, and dining on human flesh—and their connection to the most terrible night of the year was assured.

Yet vampires and werewolves were first linked to Halloween only in the twentieth century, when Hollywood filmmakers began to produce lurid representations of these myths.

ABOVE *Vampire costumes are a favorite choice for Halloween.*

Vampire classics, such as *Nosferatu* and *Dracula*, spawned numerous sequels. The werewolf genre produced *The Wolf Man*, *Wolfen*, and *An American Werewolf in London*. It has become increasingly common for such movies to be shown at Halloween screenings.

In the United States in recent years, the werewolf, the witch, and the vampire have become the predominant fancy-dress costumes for those celebrating Halloween. This gives a clear indication of their continuing power and relevance to our society.

## Fairies

*Up the airy mountain, Down the rushy glen, We daren't go a-hunting For fear of little men*

WILLIAM ALLINGHAM *THE FAIRIES*, 1850

By the Middle Ages, All Hallow's Eve was an established holiday in Britain, with a growing collection of traditions and legends. One of the most important of the newer Halloween beliefs was that malicious fairies might capture humans. The "Sidhe" (aristocratic, barrow-dwelling fairies) were notorious for their ability to place the unwary under a spell and to steal them away to their underground kingdoms. The fairies were believed to keep humans as playthings, servants, or occasionally, spouses. Anyone foolish enough to eat or drink anything

while with the fairies was unlikely ever to return home again.

Some scholars claim that prior to the fourteenth century there was no mention of

*In th' olden days of KingArthour, Of which that Britons speken grete honour, Al was this land fulfild of fayerye. The Elf-queen with hir joly compaignye Danced full often in many a grene mede*

"THE WIFE OF BATH'S TALE," *CANTERBURY TALES*

The story of Tam Lin, told in both song and poem, is one of the most well-known accounts of an escape from the fairies. Tam is held captive, but his girlfriend Janet is determined to free him from the fairies' clutches. Tam tells her how to recognize him on Samhain eve, despite the fairy spell, or "glamor":

*I'll ride on the milk-white steed,*
*And ay nearest the town;*
*Because I was an earthly knight*
*They give me that renown.*

Tam directs Janet to pull him from his fairy mount and to hold him tightly. He warns her that the fairies will change his shape, but if she holds on, he will be freed.

*They'll turn me in your arms, lady,*
*Into an esk and adder;*
*But hold me fast, and fear me not,*
*I am your bairn's father.*

Janet follows her directions, the Fairy Queen admits defeat, and Janet wins Tam back.

*Out then spak the Queen of Fairies,*
*And an angry woman was she;*
*"Shame betide her ill-far'd face,*
*And an ill death may she die,*
*For she's taen awa*
*the bonniest knight*
*In a' my companie."*

TAM LIN, TRADITIONAL

---

fairies in Britain. The Celts knew the little people and their haunts well, and credited them with an unearthly talent for deception and spite, but the earliest mention of "fairies" comes from medieval French troubadours and English poets such as Chaucer.

The English word "fairy" appears to be a distortion of the old French "faeri," itself a translation of the Latin "fata" or "fates." The fates were believed to be the three mythical beings who controlled the lives of men.

Medieval poets appear to have added these "fairies" to the existing mythology of the little people and to have embroidered details such as their tiny stature, their habit of sleeping in flowers, and their butterfly-like wings.

LEFT *The mythology of malicious fairies evolved in the Middle Ages.*

The country population of Britain were unconcerned with the origins of these superstitions, but believed in them implicitly. They simply knew their greatest fear was that, on the night of Halloween, marauding bands of fairies, known as the Host, might carry them off. In Scotland, all dreaded the "Unsellie Court," a malevolent horde of fairies who prowled the country each Samhain, intent on stealing human souls to use as servants.

As well as being the occasion on which the fairies crept around, trying to capture mortals, Halloween was also the traditional night for attempted escape by those who had been held captive in the fairy mounds. It was commonly believed that if a human embraced one of the fairies' captives and would not let go, the fairies would lose their controlling power and the captive would escape (see above).

## Halloween Witches

*I knock this rag upon this stane, To raise the wind in the Devil's name, It shal not lie, 'Til I please again!*

WITCHES' CHANT

Witches have always been credited with supernatural powers and, as a result, have long been associated with magical turning points in the year. The word "witch" originally meant "wise one." Over time, however, the meaning became corrupted and witches grew into figures of fear and detestation. Witches were believed to have the power to cause or to cure illness, to transform themselves into animals at will and, most importantly, to fly. Halloween, the ultimate night of mystery and magic, was the night when witches traditionally took to the air on broomsticks and cast their spells on the unwary.

ABOVE *Witches were believed to metamorphose into animals, such as cats or hares.*

The broomstick was the favored mode of transport for the orthodox flying witch. In Wicca, modern witches still use a broom to sweep and cleanse their magic circles. The Wiccan broom contains hidden sexual symbolism. It is traditionally made up of a shaft of "male" wood such as ash, surrounded by a besom of "female" twigs such as willow or birch. The shaft-end, hidden by the bundle of twigs, may be carved into a phallus or tipped with a phallic pine cone. Thus, the broom symbolizes the sacred, sexual joining of the God and the Goddess.

LEFT *Male witches were believed to turn into dogs or wolves.*

cats or hares while men might become dogs or, worse, wolves. There are many accounts of witches being chased and wounded in the form of hares only to carry the same injury when they returned to their human form. One of the most famous accounts of shape-shifting was given in 1662, during the trial of a young Scottish witch named Isobel Gowdie. She describes how she chanted a spell to transform herself into a cat, a hare, and a crow, then chanted another to change back.

*I sall goe intill ane haire
With sorrow and sych
and muckle caire
I sall goe in The Divellis nam
Ay while I com hom again!*

(I shall go into a hare
With sorrow and sighing
and much care
I shall go in the Devil's name
Ay, until I come home again!)

*Haire, Haire,
God send thee a black care
I was a haire just now,
I sall be in a woman's
likenes evin now!*

Scholars believe that early witches may have used a narcotic blend of herbs and fungi to commune with animal spirits and their gods. Much like modern psychotropic drugs, this preparation gave the impression of flight and came to be known as Flying Ointment.

There is debate about how it was applied, but many believe that the highly poisonous ointment was rubbed onto the wrists and ankles as a much safer alternative to ingestion, which would almost certainly have led to death. Flying Ointment is also thought to have been introduced into the vagina on the end of a phallic broomstick: the possible use of the broom in this way may have led to our modern, sexually inspired idea of witches "riding" on broomsticks.

Along with their ability to fly, witches were greatly feared for their ability to metamorphose into animals. Women were believed to favor

## Witch-Hunting

Witch-hunting swept across Europe, first in the Middle Ages and then again during the fifteenth and sixteenth centuries. The Reformation and Counter-Reformation were periods of intense political and religious disquiet across most of Europe. It is during this period of profound social upheaval that the majority of witch-hunts took place. Scholars now suggest that these "witch crazes" predominated in areas, such as border-countries, which were most affected by political turmoil and in societies where rival Christian sects were fighting for supremacy.

Germany and Switzerland, with their widespread religious instability, carried out the greatest number of witch trials, with 26,000 deaths in Germany alone. In Ireland, where the religious situation remained more stable, there were only four executions. England's strong monarchy and government meant it had comparatively little witch-hunting, the main English "witch craze" taking place during the Civil War of 1642–49 when the established order disintegrated. Throughout most of Europe, the "witch craze" died out rapidly from the middle of the seventeenth century onward.

## Scottish Witches

In Scotland 2,000 people were executed. Some of the most famous trials recorded in Scotland were those of the "Berwick Witches." These individuals are unusual among accused groups, in that they actually may have been practicing witchcraft. As their confessions were made under torture, the truth will never be known.

In 1589, one of James VI's bitterest rivals, the Fifth Earl of Bothwell, was accused of calling a Grand Sabbat of witches, covens in North Berwick. It was claimed that this group of 39 (comprising three covens of 13) had actively worked to destroy the King. James VI, who had himself written a book on witches,

ABOVE *Candles were often used by witches in spell casting.*

BELOW RIGHT *Frogs and toads feature widely in ancient witches' spells.*

*Daemonology,* was vehemently opposed to witchcraft and insisted on the harshest sentence of torture and burning at the stake for those who had been condemned.

The Berwick covens stood accused of attempting to harm James VI by magic. Supposedly led by John Fian, a local schoolteacher, the witches were charged with a variety of crimes. The first accusation was that they had raised a storm to drown the king. Under torture, several of the witches confessed that they had indeed danced to raise magical power and had tried to cause storms and high winds by throwing cats into the sea to drown them. When James VI went to Denmark to collect his fiancée, Princess Anne, serious storms at sea did interfere with his journey there and also delayed his journey back.

One of the Queen's attendants, Lady Mary Melville, was drowned on her way to meet the newlyweds, when storms sank the Burnt Island ferry in 1589.

Another of the allegations was that several members of the Berwick covens had attempted to steal some of James VI's personal clothing, in order to dress a wax "poppet" (a doll, or puppet) of the King. The witches then planned to melt the poppet over a fire: believing that, as it melted, so the King's vitality and potency would also melt away.

While there are fanciful accounts of sailing to sea in sieves and fornication with cloven-hoofed devils in the trial records, there are also precise details of how these groups may have been working together to kill the king. Witness accounts describe the "English Ambassador" giving the witches "gold to charm a toad for the hurt of the King and to hinder the issue to come of his body." Richard Graham supposedly gave Lord Bothwell instructions on how to poison the King. "He gave the said Earl some drug, willing him at some convenient time to touch therewith His Majesty's face."

The covens were only betrayed when a young serving girl, Geillis Duncan, was suspected of witchcraft by her employer David Seaton. Without a trial of any kind, Seaton had Geillis Duncan tortured until she named John Fian and many others.

ABOVE *In this engraving James I, a staunch Protestant, is depicted at the Berwick trial.*

The list of those named showed a highly unusual mix of social classes. Ordinary men and women such as Erisch Marioun, a weaver's wife, Jockie Gray-Meill, a laborer, and Janet Drummond, a servant, were listed as having worked magic alongside the well-to-do Ewfame McCalzane (Drummond's mistress), school teacher John Fian, and the respectable midwife, Agnes Sampsoune. It would have been extremely unlikely that any social interaction would have taken place between these people in ordinary circumstances. The fact that such an assortment of social classes seemed to be working together has given credence to the idea that they may actually have been members of a witches' coven.

Under the direction of James VI, all of the accused were hunted down, tortured, and then executed by burning at the stake. The Earl of Bothwell was proclaimed an outlaw for a period but, because of his elevated status, was eventually acquitted. The "Blue Stane," still in position today under the esplanade at Edinburgh Castle, marks the spot where the gruesome executions took place.

## Salem Witch-Hunts

In America, as in Europe, witches were intimately linked with Halloween and Bonfire Night. Witches were a real fear for the Puritans, and their supposed supernatural powers were taken seriously by both rich and poor. It was routine to both blame witches for illness among animals or humans and to pay them for successfully curing diseases. Witches were also believed to have the power to blight crops, transform themselves into demons, and to possess the souls of others.

America did not escape the outbreak of witch-hunting that spread across Europe in the sixteenth and seventeenth centuries. Although in Europe the witch craze ended in the middle of the seventeenth century, in America it was just beginning. In Salem, Massachusetts, a bout of witch-hunting hysteria in 1692 resulted in the arrest of more than 200 people and the death of 24.

Social and political conditions in Salem at that time could not have been more favorable for witch-hunting. There was disagreement among villagers over the delineation of town boundaries and spiritual unrest.

The family of Rev. Parris was at the center of the affair. His nine-year-old daughter, Betty, twelve-year-old niece, Abigail, and Tituba, a slave, formed a group with other village girls to try out their fortune-telling techniques. The three would would regale the girls with stories of witchcraft and demons. After several meetings, Betty and Abigail began to be frightened by Tituba's stories and started to display strange symptoms. The girls writhed in pain, hid under furniture, and complained of fevers.

In February 1692, encouraged by members of their church, the girls began to name local women as witches and to blame them for these unusual symptoms. Within three months, 200 people had been arrested on charges of witchcraft. Of those, four died in prison, 19 were hanged as witches, and one man was pressed to death under stones.

Almost as soon as it had begun, the witch-hunting craze abated. By October 1692 public opinion had changed. Increase Mather published *Cases of Conscience*, which he described as "America's first tract on evidence." In it he argued that "spectral evidence" (the description of demons that the victims claimed to have seen) should be inadmissible. He also stated "it were better that ten suspected witches should escape than one innocent person should be condemned."

At the end of 1692, Governor Phipps issued orders stating that the accused should be protected from harm. He suspended arrests of suspected witches and finally pardoned all remaining prisoners in 1693. Samuel Sewall, one of the trial judges, offered a public apology and many of the jurors confessed to being "sadly deluded and mistaken" in their decisions. A public day of "fasting and prayer for forgiveness" was held in 1697.

LEFT *Salem witch trial 1692: a "bedeviled" girl is accused.*

Susanna Martin was a witch who lived in Amesbury
With brilliant eye and saucy tongue she worked her sorcery
And when into the judges court the sheriffs brought her hither
The lilacs drooped as she passed by And then were seen to wither

A witch she was, though trim and neat with comely head held high
It did not seem that one as she with Satan so would vie
And when in court th' afflicted ones proclaimed her evil ways
She laughed aloud and boldly then Met Cotton Mathers' gaze

"Who hath bewitched these maids," he asked, and strong was her reply
"If they be dealing in black arts, ye know as well as I"
And then the stricken ones made moan as she approached near
They saw her shape upon the beam So none could doubt 'twas there

The neighbors 'round swore to the truth of her Satanic powers
That she could fly o'er land and stream and come dry shod through showers
At night, twas said, she had appeared a cat of fearsome mien
"Avoid the she-devil," they cried, to keep their spirits clean

The spectral evidence was weighed, then stern the parson spoke
"Thou shalt not suffer a witch to live, 'tis written in the Book"
Susanna Martin so accused, spoke with flaming eyes
"I scorn these things for they are naught But filthy gossips' lies"

Now those bewitched, they cried her out, and loud their voice did ring
They saw a bird above her head, an evil yellow thing
And so, beneath a summer sky, Susanna Martin died
And still in scorn she faced the rope Her comely head held high

Susanna Martin was a witch who lived in Amesbury
With brilliant eye and saucy tongue she worked her sorcery
And when into the judges court the sheriffs brought her hither
The lilacs drooped as she passed by And then were seen to wither.

# Vampires

The vampire myth is an ancient one. Many cultures have legends of the "undead"—beings that return from the grave to feed on the blood of the living. The idea of vampirism may have originated in Asia, where there are early accounts of vampire foxes and blood-drinking ogres, but the myth really took root when it reached the Orthodox Christian countries of Eastern Europe. Bulgaria, Romania, Hungary, and, most notoriously, Transylvania, had a particularly fertile culture of vampires and vampire-hunting until the nineteenth century.

Vampire activity was traditionally signaled by the sudden death of animals, neighbors, and, finally, of relatives. One well-documented case is that of the sexagenarian Peter Plogojowitz, who, in 1732, though officially dead, was recorded as having visited his son to ask for food. On being turned away, he was believed to have killed his son and neighbors in order to drink their blood.

At that time, almost anything was believed to cause an individual to become a vampire. Being born with a birth caul or teeth; being conceived on an inauspicious day or out of wedlock; being the seventh child or the child of a mother who did not eat salt or garlic, were all sure signs of vampire tendencies.

It was commonplace for corpses to be exhumed at regular intervals to check for any developing signs of vampirism. Indications of guilt included blood around the mouth, a foot pointing into a corner of the coffin, or a bloated appearance.

Corpses could be staked in the traditional manner, through the heart, but there were many other methods of dealing with suspected vampires. Bodies could be destroyed by beheading, burning, boiling water, holy water, garlic in the mouth, or exorcism. Some vampire-hunters shot a bullet into the coffin for good measure. Gypsies, now known as

ABOVE *Vlad III Tepes, known as Dracula, inspired Bram Stoker's famous novel.*

RIGHT *A castle in Transylvania, the notorious land of vampires.*

Romanies, preferred to stab the suspected vampire in the heart and eyes with iron pins, to stake the body through both legs, and to complete the process by tucking a sprig of hawthorn into the vampire's sock.

Perhaps the most celebrated vampire case was that of farmer Arnold Paole, which caused widespread debate at the time. Paole was believed to have been attacked by a vampire in his youth and on his death, to have turned into a vampire himself. Documents record a spree in which he murdered and drank the blood of several of his neighbors. Western scholars such as the theologian Dom Augustine Calmet (who published his famous treatise on vampires in 1746) began to raise the possibility that vampirism was a reality. Others refuted the idea and laws were passed to prevent rural populations from digging up their dead.

Bram Stoker published *Dracula* in 1897, creating the defining image of the vampire: aristocratic, but ultimately degenerate. Stoker based his novel on the historical figure Voivode Vlad III Tepes (known as Dracula), a Prince of Wallachia from 1456 to 1462. Vlad's father had already built such a reputation for bloodthirstiness that he was known as Dracul—the Dragon, or Devil. Vlad III, was dubbed Dracula—Son of the Devil, a name he liked and used. Vlad III lived up to his name and, because of his delight in torturing and staking to death his enemies, earned a grisly soubriquet of his own, Tepes—The Impaler.

Anecdotal evidence describes Vlad Dracula putting entire cities to death by impaling them on stakes. On one occasion 10,000 people were killed in Brasov, Transylvania, creating "a forest of the dying." Accounts record Dracula setting up dining tables among the bodies and picnicking.

PART ONE

# Werewolves

*Even a man who is pure at heart
And says his prayers at night. Can
become a wolf when the wolfbane
blooms. And the Moon is full and bright*

CURT SIODAMAK, *THE WOLF MAN*
UNIVERSAL PICTURES, 1941

The werewolf myth is as widespread and as ancient as that of the vampire. One of the oldest accounts of the wolf-man appears nearly two thousand years ago in Ovid's *Metamorphoses* (c.17 C.E.) The poet tells the Greek myth of King Lycaon who served a feast of human flesh to Zeus, and was then changed by the god into a wolf and banished from his kingdom.

Men with the ability to transform themselves into wolves at will were revered as

BELOW *Like vampires, werewolves were viewed as bloodthirsty and degenerate.*

powerful shamans in early Nordic, Siberian, and Native American cultures. These societies accepted shape-shifting as traditional magical practice. Assuming the identity of a wolf was seen as a way for human hunters to commune with animal hunters, for the tribe to learn more about their prey, and to come to terms with the horror, blood, and possible guilt of a kill.

## The Werewolf Myth

In Western Europe, werewolves were feared and reviled as men who had betrayed their humanity and surrendered to the baser instincts of blood lust, sexual depravity, and greed. In the early Middle Ages, the idea of the ravening werewolf was synonymous with Satan's power on Earth: anyone suspected of being a werewolf was assumed to be in Satan's thrall.

There are numerous accounts of werewolf sightings and trials. One of the most notorious cases was that of the German, Stubbe Peeter, a suspected werewolf who was convicted and executed on October 31, 1590.

Stubbe Peeter was accused of incest, rape, and murder. A contemporary account of his life claimed he had "destroyed and spoiled an unknown number of men, women, and children, as well as sheep, lambs, goats, and cattle." Peeter was believed to own a belt of wolf skin, which, when worn, enabled him to become a wolf.

## The Wolf and the Moon

The werewolf myth is not defined by any one classic piece of literature. Because of this, our approach to the myth has continued to change subtly over time. In early literature, the werewolf was originally used as an allegory for evil, a way of examining those parts of human behavior that society found most unacceptable.

The wolf is a nocturnal hunter. It is often heard howling at the moon and, like most hunters, it preys on the weakest members of

a flock or herd. By its association with darkness and the shadows, the wolf came to be seen as a sinister animal, a creature of the night. It is significant that we continue to choose the wolf as a way of representing our deepest fears about ourselves and our baser instincts.

More recently, as a result of the quantity of films dealing with werewolves, we have come to view the man-wolf in a more sympathetic light. In *The Wolf Man* Lon Chaney Jr. gave a landmark portrayal of the werewolf who, while in human form, feels anguish and remorse for the crimes he

ABOVE *The myth of the werewolf is associated with the full moon.*

committed as a wolf. Later werewolf allegories, such as *Wolfen* and *Wolf*, portray the werewolf with some compassion.

No matter how well disposed we become to the Hollywood screen wolf-man, most of us still retain a visceral fear of the power of darkness to make us less than human. The werewolf remains an archetypal symbol for humanity's deepest fears, and as such it is an entirely appropriate Halloween monster.

THE PRESENT

# TRADITIONAL HALLOWEEN GAMES

UNTIL VERY RECENTLY, winter was the period of greatest hardship for much of the population. The weather was bitterly cold, food was scarce, and death from starvation was a real danger. These fears, combined with the widespread belief that supernatural spirits and wandering souls were at large, made Halloween night a terrifying time.

Old Halloween games all contained elements of risk, danger, and fear. They provided an unconscious way of ritualizing and lessening the power of the things that scared people most. If players survived the ordeal implicit in the games, they were rewarded with a prize and a rush of adrenaline that reaffirmed they were alive and well and would live through another winter.

Apple Bobbing, for example, forced players to move physically from one realm to another. Just as the soul left its earthly existence and crossed the water to the Underworld, so players risked leaving the comfort of the ordinary world to plunge their heads under potentially life-threatening water. The reward was laughter and high spirits, which drove back the darkness, as well as an apple, fruit of the immortals, which promised safe passage to the "summer lands." Hanch Apple, an alternative quest game also based on risk, had players braving the test of fire to snatch a bite of the magical fruit.

Modern Halloween games have changed only slightly. While we no longer like to expose ourselves to any real, physical danger, we actively seek out games in which we can experience the fear of the unexpected. Many modern games, such as Body Parts, revolve around players, often blindfolded, having to touch substances that are slimy or unpleasant in some way. This is usually accompanied by a horror story in which various blood-soaked organs are described at length.

BELOW *Like many Halloween games, The Treacle Bannock has ancient origins.*

ABOVE *In the past, players would try to snatch a bite of an apple as it spun. Over the years, the candles were extinguished and eventually replaced for safety's sake.*

GAMES

## Snap Apple or Hanch Apple

This game, not for the faint-hearted, was once played outside by adults, who tied two light pieces of wood together to form a cross. The cross, in turn, was suspended horizontally from the branch of a tree or a barn door. The candles were lit and the cross was set spinning. Those who were daring enough tried to take a bite out of the apples as they spun past. Early accounts of this game always warned players to be careful not to get burned.

Today, marshmallows dunked in gooey syrup or coated with sticky peanut butter are used instead of the candles for a messy, fun-filled game.

Another less perilous version of this game, which children enjoy today, has apples tied to strings and suspended from a doorway. The children then have to eat the apple with their hands behind their backs.

GAMES

## The Treacle Bannock

This is a Scottish version of the same game, using cornbread instead of apples. It is particularly good for younger children because it is extremely messy. Bannocks (pieces of cornbread) are heavily coated with molasses or corn syrup and then suspended on strings. Players have to eat them while keeping their hands behind their backs. This game inevitably results in molasses all over the faces of the players. A coin can be placed in the middle as a prize.

GAMES

## Snap Dragon

Here's another game from the past played strictly by daring adults, who needed to exercise extreme care. A batch of Snap Dragon raisins (see recipe on page 94) first had to be prepared.

ABOVE *A traditional Halloween game involved snatching heated raisins.*

On Halloween night, a large, flat, flame-resistant plate was placed in the oven until it was warm to the touch. A number of Snap Dragon raisins (4 to 5 per player) were put on the plate. A ladle full of brandy (or whiskey) was heated over a very low gas ring or candle, until blue vapor started to rise. The brandy was then lit and poured over the raisins on the plate.

Adult daredevils tried to snatch as many raisins as they could from the plate, being careful not to burn themselves. For obvious reasons, this dangerous game is no longer played today.

GAMES

## The Priest's Cat

In the eighteenth century, children played a game of forfeits around the bonfire. From the dying embers they would choose a branch that still had a bright, glowing tip and then pass it

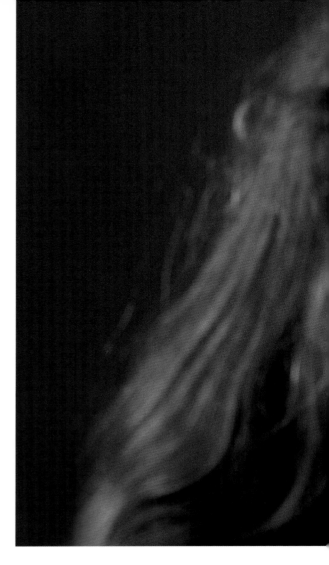

from person to person. As they passed the branch around, the children would chant:

*About wi' that, About wi' that
Keep alive the priest's cat*

The aim of the game was to avoid being caught with the branch when the tip stopped glowing. Whoever was unlucky enough to hold the "dead cat" had to perform a forfeit such as singing a song or reciting a poem. The death of a priest's cat was considered particularly unlucky by country people, because the cat's

GAMES

## The Three Luggies

Like many Halloween games, this one tries to determine what the future has in store. There are several versions. One Scottish version uses three bowls, filled with earth, milk, and dirty water respectively. The blindfolded player moves forward to choose a bowl. Earth means a death in the family; milk means a contented family life; and the dirty water, a life of spinster- or bachelorhood. In Ireland, the same game was played using earth, a ring,

ABOVE *In The Three Luggies, the blindfolded player chooses his fate.*

spirit was believed to transform itself into a witch, who would then haunt the village.

A nineteenth-century version of the Priest's Cat called Jack's-Alive was played indoors. Children passed a lighted taper with the words:

*Jack's alive and likely to live*
*If he dies in your hand, you've*
*a forfeit to give.*

GLOSSARY OF SHEFFIELD WORDS,
SIDNEY ADDEY, 1888

and a set of rosary beads. The earth meant a death; the ring, romance or an ongoing happy marriage; and the beads, a single life of solemn, religious contemplation.

This game can easily be adapted for children with coins symbolizing future wealth, hearts holding the promise of future romance, and candies for good luck.

# MODERN HALLOWEEN GAMES

## Body Parts

This game needs a bit of advance planning. Decide on which organs you are going to describe, then collect and prepare the ingredients (see right). On the night of your Halloween party, rig up an old sheet across one end of the room and cut the appropriate number of slits in it (one for each body part). Make sure the slits are very small so that players can't see through. Place the various ingredients on stools or chairs so that players can reach them through the curtain. Then tell a story describing, in lurid terms, an operation that has gone horribly wrong. Invite your players to come up and identify the body parts. The aim of the game is, of course, to make players feel as squeamish as possible.

## Nice or Nasty

A milder alternative for younger children has several boxes marked Nice or Nasty. The boxes have small holes cut in the side so that children can put their hands in to discover the contents. Make sure everyone experiences the Nasty boxes first. These could contain piles of plastic spiders, worms, and snakes, bowls of brains or intestines (see Body Parts)—or simply crumpled-up cellophane, which crackles loudly and feels surprisingly prickly. The Nice box could contain candies, soft toys, and trinkets for the children to keep.

## Unlucky Dip

Here's another extremely messy game that young children will enjoy. Fill a small plastic trash can with cold, cooked oatmeal. The oatmeal needs to be fairly liquid so that it doesn't go completely solid when cold. You can dye the oatmeal with food coloring to make it look even more unappealing—red, green, or black are wonderful Halloween choices. Seal candies and toys in small plastic bags and push these to the bottom of the pail. Invite children

| ORGANS FOR BODY PARTS GAME | |
|---|---|
| Brain | Cold, cooked cauliflower, coated with oil |
| Eyes | Peeled grapes, olives, or canned lychees |
| Tongue | Half a peeled avocado |
| Intestines | String of raw sausages coated with oil |
| | Cold cooked spaghetti or other noodles mixed with custard |
| Liver | Balloon half-filled with water and coated with cooking oil |
| Broken arm | Sleeve of an old sweater stuffed so it feels solid. The broken bone is made by pushing a broken, celery stalk through the sweater, (exposing plenty of stringy ends for sinews), then coating the exposed end liberally with "blood." |
| Fingers | Carrots boiled in their skins |
| Blood | Corn syrup with added red food coloring, strawberry sauce, ketchup |

to feel around in the slime and try to reach for one of the plastic-wrapped prizes. To make the slime even more revolting, layer it with cold custard dyed green with food coloring.

GAMES

# Bobbing for Apples, or Apple Dookin

People don't realize when they plunge their heads underwater and try to bite a wildly bobbing apple that they are re-enacting one of the solemn rites of passage of the ancient Celts. The Ordeal of Water was an epic, spiritual journey undertaken in search of esoteric knowledge. The journey involved a quest for the mysterious Avalon, the Apple Isle—home of immortality and hidden wisdom. The quest itself was a metaphor for the soul's descent into the Underworld, while the apple, symbolic fruit of the all-knowing Triple Goddess, was a passport to the world of the dead. If the questor were lucky enough to find the fruit of immortality, he would gain the knowledge which would help his soul to live forever.

All you need to play this game is a large tub, or bath, filled with water, in which you float several apples. Players, in turn, try to bite an apple out of the water while keeping their hands behind their backs. It's much harder than it looks!

GAMES

# Children of the Night

This bloodthirsty game is an adaptation of the childhood classic "Murder in the Dark." You need a fairly large group of people: an odd number is better than an even number, but not absolutely necessary. There should be a minimum number of nine players.

You need a card for each player, on which his or her role is written down. The majority of the players will be the Angry Mob, but one player will be the Burghermeister (or Mayor), one will be Dr. Van Helsing, and two players will be "vampires."

The cards are shuffled and dealt face down so that each player has one. Everyone can look at their own card but must keep it a secret from the others. Only the Burghermeister announces himself and takes charge of the game. The two vampires keep their identities secret, as does Van Helsing.

The game is played in two locations: the village at night, and the castle crypt by day.

## How to Play

1 Beginning at night, the Burghermeister directs all the players to close their eyes and sleep. He then says, "Vampires, open your eyes." The two vampires obey his command, and recognize one another.

2 The Burghermeister then says to the vampires, "Vampires, Children of the Night, choose your victim."

3 The vampires select their target in silence; their main concern is not to attract the attention of the rest of the villagers sitting next to them. They signal their choice of victim to the Burghermeister as quietly and discreetly as possible. When they have made their choice clear, the Burghermeister says, "Vampires, close your eyes."

4 He then says, "Dr. Van Helsing, open your eyes and choose someone to investigate."

5 Whoever holds the Van Helsing card then opens his eyes and looks around. He silently chooses a player and the Burghermeister silently indicates whether that player is a vampire or an innocent villager. It is in Van Helsing's interest to be as quiet as possible so the sleeping vampires will not be able to detect his identity.

6 When Van Helsing has had an answer about his chosen player, the Burghermeister says, "Close your eyes and sleep."

7 He then says, "It is day and we are in the castle crypt. Everyone open your eyes."

8 The Burghermeister points to the vampires' chosen victim and announces that this player was found dead on the outskirts of the village during the night. The player shows his card, revealing his identity. He can no longer speak or take part in the discussions.

9 The Angry Mob now want revenge and decide whom they will stake through the

LEFT *The actor Bela Lugosi played many famous vampire roles.*

ABOVE *The bloodthirsty Children of the Night is a good game for a Halloween party.*

heart. Any member of the mob can voice an opinion. Van Helsing will try to give as many clues about his suspicions as possible. He will not reveal his true identity. He knows that if he does, when night falls, the vampires will kill him. The two vampires will, of course, want to remain incognito and will try to blame an innocent villager for their crime.

10 When a majority choice is made, that player is "staked." He then reveals his identity and takes no further part in the game.

11 After every staking, night falls and the cycle begins again. The vampires choose a victim, and Van Helsing has another

opportunity to identify the vampires. The following day in the crypt, the Burghermeister identifies the corpse and the Angry Mob decide whom they will stake next.

The vampires win if they reduce the population to two (or one, if only one vampire survives). The Angry Mob win if they kill both vampires. You can adapt this game as you choose and it works well over dinner with a Halloween feast (see pages 92–103 for recipes).

# TRADITIONAL HALLOWEEN TRICKS

HALLOWEEN, OR "MISCHIEF NIGHT," was one of the few occasions in the year when children could be as naughty as they liked. Tricks were expected by adults and, in the main, taken in good humor. If adults were foolish enough to become angry about the pranks played on them, they guaranteed worse mischief-making for the rest of the night.

One of the possible origins of the American tradition of trick-or-treat was the fact that many adults anticipated Halloween raids on their kitchens. They made sure there was a good supply of cakes, pies, and candies, readily accessible by open doors and windows for the various groups of children to steal. By providing edible booty, the householder ensured that the tricks played on him would not be too annoying.

In the United States, the tradition became refined to the point where the threat of a trick was made unless the homeowner first made the promise of a treat.

### TRICKS
## Burnin' the Reeky Mehr

This was a much-loved routine among younger children in the eighteenth and nineteenth centuries, because it provided the maximum amount of upheaval and annoyance with the minimum effort. The trickster hollowed out a cabbage stalk or "custock," and then filled it with slightly damp sheep's wool. This was set on fire, creating a lot of thick smoke. One end of the stalk was placed against the keyhole of the victim's door and the trickster then blew hard, with the result that the house was instantly filled with thick, evil-smelling smoke.

### TRICKS
## Brackin' Glaice

This was a favorite among rowdy gangs of Scottish and Irish youths at the end of the nineteenth century and is still played on Halloween to this day in Scotland.

Two boys run up to the window of an unsuspecting victim. The first boy starts hammering on the window and shouting. When the hammering reaches a crescendo, the

LEFT *Trick-or-treaters are rewarded with candy or chocolate.*

second boy drops an empty bottle. The victim thinks his windows have been broken and rushes outside. He is confronted with lots of broken glass, but, to his relief, is left with his windows still intact.

## TRICKS
### Dirlin' on Windies

Children in the northeast of Scotland were great exponents of this particular Halloween caper in the 1920s.

First, they prepared their weapons by banging nails and pins into empty, wooden cotton spools. Next, they fitted a pencil into

ABOVE *The tradition of playing mischievous tricks on Halloween is an old one.*

the center of the spool and wound a length of string around the whole contraption. The spools were placed against the windows of a victim's house and held in position with the pencil. Then the string was pulled sharply. As the string unwound, the spool revolved and the nails and pins made an extremely loud rattle against the window.

The final part of the trick involved the children dodging out of sight as quickly as possible to avoid the angry homeowner.

# MODERN HALLOWEEN TRICKS

### TRICKS

## The Halloween Psychic Challenge

This is a great way to convince your friends that you really do have the gift of second sight and is best done at a Halloween party.

First you need an accomplice, chosen and prepared in advance. It's better to sort this out before the party.

Next, encourage your friends (including the accomplice) to go into another room and choose a number between one and ten. To add to the drama, you can insist that an unbiased observer stays with you to make sure you are not trying to listen at the door. When the group has decided on a number, tell them to open the door and stand in a circle.

Go from person to person in turn. Hold each person's face between both of your hands and, silently, look deep into their eyes. Make a big play of concentrating hard and try to

ABOVE *Impress your friends with your "psychic" powers.*

LEFT *Halloween is a time for dressing up as your favorite character, scary or otherwise.*

unnerve each of them with the depth and intensity of your stare. Make sure you hold each person's face for at least ten seconds.

Your accomplice will have been primed on what to do. When you reach him and place your hands on his face, he will very gently clench his jaw the same number of times as the number chosen. For example, the number five means five tiny jaw clenches. If done gently enough, these tiny movements are completely invisible, especially in candlelight.

Hold every face in turn and then amaze everyone by getting the number right. If you are not sure of the number, simply go around the circle a second time until you reach your accomplice, who will indicate the number to you secretly once again.

To make things even more unbelievable for your friends, you could tell your accomplice to suggest that the group choose a number higher than ten to deliberately confuse your psychic powers. Make sure the number is not too high, maybe 12 or 13, as your accomplice will still have to relay the number to by means of jaw-clenches.

When you go from face to face, pretend to be disorientated and unable to understand what's happening. After you have been to each in turn, and your accomplice has told you the answer, make a speech about how your psychic powers never normally let you down, but on this occasion you are getting the number 12. When your friends demand the trick again, which they will, do it once more and then claim to be exhausted. This trick works every time.

TRICKS

## The Haunted Muffin

This trick needs a little advance preparation and reasonable skill on your part to avoid detection. First, choose a pale-colored cake or muffin. Cut it in half carefully, as you will have to reassemble it later. Mix up some food coloring to make a convincing "baked-brown" color and then thin this out with water until it is very faint. Carefully paint the outline of an evil-looking demon, ghost, or skull and crossbones onto one half of the muffin and let it dry completely. Simple shapes will look most convincing. You may want to paint over the design with another coat of color until you have exactly the right "baked" look. Reassemble the muffin.

ABOVE *The better your artistic skills, the more convincing The Haunted Muffins.*

Keep the muffin with you in your pocket until you are with a group of people, preferably in a dimly lit Halloween party. While your friends are helping themselves to appetizers and their attention is distracted, slip the muffin onto your plate. Pretend to cut it in half and then reel back in horror as you see the demon in the bun. The host of the party will, of course, deny all knowledge of such a prank and, provided you continue to act as if genuinely horrified, your friends will be unnerved. In true Halloween spirit, never admit to having baked the bun.

## TRICKS
# Bedroom–Bathroom Horrors

Easy but effective, this trick unfolds in several parts, becoming progressively more messy and annoying for the victim. You can adjust the level of potential horror, depending on the tolerance of your friends and family.

First, lay the trap. Get up before anyone else is awake and quietly tie together all the bedroom doorknobs with a long piece of string. Don't tie the string too tightly because you do want your family to escape (eventually). Next, go into the bathroom and substitute the ordinary bathroom soap for black-ink soap from a joke store.

If you want your trick to be remembered forever, lift the toilet seat and stretch a piece of plastic wrap over the bowl. Do this meticulously, so that the plastic wrap is virtually invisible. Lower the toilet seat, completing the illusion. Think for some time about going through with this part of the trick —some people may not find it funny and you may be the one who has to clean up the consequences! Finally, close the bathroom door

and coat the handle with a generous amount of butter or petroleum jelly.

When your family wakes up, there will be great confusion as they try to release themselves from their bedrooms. The first person to escape will stumble to the bathroom but be unable to open the door because the handle is slippery. They will finally make it into the bathroom and try to wash their greasy hands, but will cover themselves with black ink. With luck, they will notice the plastic wrap across the toilet; if not ... well, it will be a Halloween to remember!

ABOVE *Tie all the bedroom doorknobs together with string.*

LEFT *Black ink soap: the more you wash, the dirtier you get.*

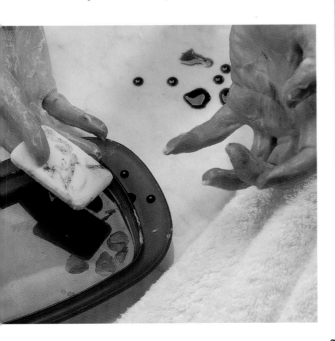

# CRAFTS

### INTRODUCE THE SPIRIT

*of Halloween into your home
by trying new crafts, learning
and casting spells, having
fun with decorations, and
discovering traditional recipes.*

CRAFTS

## Creating Your Own
## Dark Mirror

Dark mirrors, or skrying glasses, are
traditionally used at Samhain for divination.
They can be used to look into the future, to
contact the ancestors, or simply as a meditation
aid, helping to clear and focus the mind. They
are simple, cheap, and quick to make.

You will need a piece of round glass: a
glazier or picture-framing shop will cut glass to
whatever size you want. A diameter of 5 or 7
inches (13 or 18 cm) works best. Ask the glass-
cutter to bevel the edges, which makes the
glass safe to handle.

You will also need a circular piece of
wood that is 2 inches (5 cm) larger than the
diameter of your glass. This could be pine,
which is very cheap, or oak or walnut, which
is extremely expensive. Any lumberyard will be
able to cut the wood to your specifications.
Sand down the edges of your wooden disk
until they are smooth. In order to decorate
your mirror you will also need black spray
paint, pencils, beads or seeds, watercolor or
acrylic paints, and clear, strong glue.

1 Prepare and cleanse your workspace. Position your
glass in the center of the base and draw around it
lightly with a pencil.

4 Let the glue dry, then decorate the wooden base
however you like. Avoid using a varnish to set the
decoration as the glossy surface detracts from the shine
of the mirror. You will find that as the decoration wears
away, your mirror takes on a beautifully aged look.

2 Next, paint one side of your glass black. This is most easily done with spray paint, which gives an even coat. Don't be tempted to touch the glass. Let it dry and then give it a second coat of paint. You are aiming for a flawless black finish on one side of the glass only

3 When the paint is completely dry, you can mount your dark mirror onto its base. Use a strong, clear glue or an epoxy resin and apply liberally to the wooden base, keeping well inside the circle you have drawn. Carefully position the glass, paint side down, over the glue: this is the only delicate part of the whole process.

5 Consecrate your dark mirror with salt and water using the instructions on the following page.

6 When your mirror is complete, wrap it in a black cloth and keep it in a safe, private place.

### CONSECRATING YOUR MIRROR

Cast a circle in the usual way. Sprinkle the mirror with the salt water, saying: "May the powers of Earth and Water fill this glass, that I may see clearly." Pass the mirror briefly through the candle flame and incense smoke saying: "May the powers of Fire and Air fill this glass, that I may see clearly."

Never expose your mirror to any light, except candlelight or firelight—keep it wrapped in black silk or in a black bag made of cotton, silk, or wool.

If you want to try skrying without a mirror, fill a black, glazed bowl with spring water.

## Using Your Dark Mirror

° After sunset on the night of Samhain or Halloween, cast a circle of protection (see pages 106–7) using a violet candle.

° Let your mind become still and clear.

° Unwrap your mirror carefully and hold it or position it in such a way that the candle flame is reflected in the glass.

° Decide whether you hope to see the future, encounter the ancestors, or simply meditate. Say: "As the year turns, as I sit at summer's end and winter's dawning, may I share the wisdom and clear sight of the Great Ones."

° Once again, still your mind and relax thoroughly, letting your thoughts drift.

° You may begin to see shapes or symbols flickering in the mirror's darkness.

° When you feel you have seen enough, put away your mirror and thank the powers of Earth, Air, Fire, and Water for their help.

° Make sure that you eat and drink something after your meditation, as this will ground you and bring you back to the everyday world.

RIGHT *Try to relax your mind, and look deeply into your dark mirror.*

CRAFTS

## "Good Luck Come to Me" Bags

In many magical traditions, witches and shamans made up little skin or cloth bags to hold magical talismans. These could be used to draw good luck to the recipient or to ward off bad luck. They were worn next to the skin, and became more powerful as they became impregnated with human sweat.

TO MAKE YOUR OWN GOOD LUCK BAGS
YOU WILL NEED:

A piece of red or gold wool, silk, or cotton
Red thread for sewing
Red cord to make drawstrings
"Good Luck" seed mix
Charms such as coins, hearts, or flowers

"GOOD LUCK" SEED MIX

1 tsp apple seeds
1 tsp coriander seeds
1 tsp dried whole cloves
1 tsp dried angelica seeds
1 nutmeg
1 hazelnut (in its shell)
1 tsp crushed cinnamon bark

BELOW *"Go Away" seed ingredients, ready to mix and place in a bag.*

CRAFTS

## "Go Away" Bags

TO MAKE YOUR OWN GO AWAY BAG
YOU WILL NEED:

A black drawstring bag (see right)
"Go Away" protection mix
Paper and pencil
A ball of black wool

"GO AWAY" PROTECTION MIX

1 tsp dried fennel seeds
1 tsp dried poppy seeds
1 tsp dried caraway seeds
1 tsp dried lemon seeds
1 tbsp whole star anise
1 whole head of garlic

IMPORTANT: *Never use magic as a first option if you have a problem. Instead, try all the usual channels (communication, treatment, negotiation, and so on) for dealing with it. These protection bags should not be used under any circumstances against other people. It is possible to make one for someone else if they ask for your help. Remember, if you should be foolish enough to consider using magic against another person, your own plans will invariably go awry.*

° Make up your bag as per the instructions on the right, and fill it with "Go Away" mix.
° Decide on what you want protection from, for example a phobia or fear, or pain associated with an illness or accident. Write this on a piece of paper and add this to the bag.
° Seal the bag tightly and knot it shut.
° Wind a piece of black wool tightly around the sealed bag, and knot again.
° Protect and purify your bag with Earth, Air, Fire, and Water as usual.
° Bury it far away from your home. Dig a deep hole so it will remain undisturbed.
° Witches believe that as the bag rots away, so your fear or pain will diminish.

1 Cut out a rectangle of material 6 x 2½ inches (15 x 7 cm). Fold in half and sew up the two open sides to make a bag 3 x 2 inches (9 x 7 cm) long. Take two lengths of cord about 8–10 inches (20–25 cm) long. Double each cord in half and tie the loose ends to make two circles 4–5 inches (10–13 cm) across.

2 Position the cords so that the two circles overlap. Make sure that each of the knotted ends remains opposite the other. This is essential so that you can draw the top of your bag together. Place the cords along the top of your bag and fold a hem over them. Carefully sew the hem down, ensuring that you allow enough space to enable you to pull the drawstrings tight.

3 Turn your bag inside out. Fill your bag with "Good Luck" seed mix. Add anything else you wish, such as a coin for luck with money, red heart or a dried red rose for luck in love, and a bean or some dried fruit, for contentment.

4 Knot the cord ends together tightly, sealing the bag. Purify and protect your bag by thanking the powers of Earth, Air, Fire, and Water as usual. You can either keep it for yourself or give it to a friend. Place the bag under your pillow from one full moon until the next.

CRAFTS

# The Garland of Knowledge

The apple has always been seen, in Western magical traditions, as the fruit of the Underworld. To the Celts, it was the Silver Bough and to eat its fruit was to receive the knowledge of the ancient ones and, as a result, immortality.

If you cut an apple horizontally you will reveal the secret within it: a five-pointed star, emblem of the Goddess. Romany Gypsies call it the Star of Knowledge and revere it as a sign of great power. They use the Star in love charms and spells to bring good luck and long life.

At the apple's heart are the seeds. Cut through their centers, each resembles the great mystery of the female body, the womb. Early Christians were so appalled at this "sinful" sight that they made the practice of cutting an apple horizontally a virtual taboo. This tradition has lasted to the present day and most people still cut an apple vertically, from top to bottom, so destroying the star.

TO MAKE A GARLAND OF KNOWLEDGE
YOU WILL NEED:

About eight bright red apples (preferably those
with pale white flesh)
Lemon juice
Wax paper
A hot glue gun or strong, clear adhesive
A thin sheet of cardboard
Some red and silver ribbons

## Using the Garland

Your finished Garland of Knowledge can be hung in any room where you read, study, spell cast, or meditate. On Samhain itself, the apple garland can be hung above any divination work you plan to do and will inspire your efforts, particularly if you hope to contact your ancestors.

BELOW *An alternative Garland of Knowledge, made with whole apples.*

1 First, slice the apples horizontally as finely as possible, trying to make the slices wafer-thin. Dip them in lemon juice to ensure they stay white. Next, cover a flat baking sheet with wax paper and lay the apple rings out so that they do not touch. You may need several sheets of wax paper.

2 Place the apple rings in an oven, and prop the door open, then bake on the lowest possible heat for two or three hours. It is essential that the door is open so that any steam can escape and the apples dry thoroughly. Alternatively, place the apple rings on wire trays and put them in a pantry or shady, dry room until they have dried out completely.

3 When the apple rings are completely dry, you can create your garland. Prepare and cleanse your workspace as usual. Cut a ring of stiff cardboard—its size depends on the number of apple slices you have. Make sure the width of the ring is less than that of your smallest apple slice. Choose the most perfect slices for the front of the garland and set them aside.

4 Glue the remaining apple slices onto the back of the cardboard ring, creating a layer of overlapping stars. It's better to start with the back to get some practice at positioning and gluing. Glue the reserved slices to the front of the garland in the same way. Finish your garland with a decorative hanging loop of red and silver ribbons.

CRAFTS

## The Need Fire

The ancient Celts believed that a Need Fire could be used to produce magical results, but that it should only be used in times of great necessity (hence the name). Samhain was a traditional time for the Need Fire because winter was beginning, food was scarce, and the impending cold often proved deadly.

Need Fires had to be lit without the use of iron to make sparks, since iron was believed to lessen magical power. The Celts either traveled until they found a fire that had started as the result of lightning striking a tree, or made a fire using only wood. Some sources state that Need Fires were only ever lit on an island surrounded by fresh water. The resulting wild fire, or living fire, was believed to be especially magical and would act as a protection for those who made it.

Lighting a fire without a flint or matches is hard work and undeniably difficult, but it is possible and the end result is truly magical.

TO CREATE YOUR OWN SAMHAIN NEED FIRE YOU WILL HAVE TO FIND:

| | |
|---|---|
| A spindle: | A straight twig of hard wood (such as oak) about 1 foot (30 cm) long |
| A bow: | A second branch, about 2–3 feet long (60–90 cm) and 1 inch (2.5 cm) in diameter |
| A socket: | A small piece of hard wood, which fits your hand comfortably |
| A fireboard: | A flat piece of soft wood (such as pine) about 1 foot long (30 cm) |
| Tinder: | This must be bone-dry and can be straw, old wood shavings, dried grass, sawdust, or even fluffed-up absorbent cotton |
| Kindling: | Small, dry, dead twigs |
| Fuel: | Dry, dead wood, grease, string |

If you practice, you will be able to create fire using nothing but the wood itself. You can use this technique to provide a light for your Halloween bonfire, ensuring protection for yourself and your family for the year ahead.

1 Sharpen one end of your spindle to a blunt point. Hollow a little indentation in the socket piece and rub this with grease to prevent friction. Carve a small hollow in the fireboard next to one edge and then cut a little downward-pointing, V-shaped nick, from the edge of the wood to the middle of the hollow. The upside-down V acts as a knife-edge, shaving away the end of the spindle as it heats up and becomes burning charcoal.

2 Make a bow by bending the two ends of the second twig and tying them with string. Place some tinder under the hole in the fireboard and kneel on the other end of the fireboard.

3 Loop the bowstring once around the spindle and put the point of the spindle into the hole in the fireboard. Hold the spindle in place using the socket piece. You need to press down fairly hard to keep the spindle in place. Spin the spindle with long, easy strokes of the bow, until smoke starts to appear. Keep spinning until thicker smoke appears. The hot powder (burning charcoal) that is produced can be blown until it glows red.

4 Roll some fluffy tinder around the ember until it catches light. Transfer your lighted tinder to a prepared pile of tinder and kindling.

Note: Our word "tinder" is a corruption of the ancient Ogham word for holly, "tinne," which meant fire. Holly is such a dense, dry wood that it will burn when it is still green (i.e. newly cut).

CRAFTS
# Pumpkin Lanterns

No one really knows why people started hollowing out vegetable lanterns for Halloween. Some suggest that the ancient Celts used a hollow turnip to carry an ember from the central Samhain fire back to their hearths to rekindle the New Year's flame. Others claim that frightening faces were carved onto lanterns and turned to face the window in order to scare away the evil spirits that were loose on All Hallow's eve. Certainly, until the middle of the twentieth century children in Scotland and the North of England carried hollow turnip lanterns, hung on string handles, to light their way as they went guising or trick-or-treating.

The many Irish and Scottish immigrants who moved to America took the tradition of carving turnip lanterns with them. Turnips were hard to find in America and so pumpkins, which were more readily available, were substituted. As they tended to be much larger, pumpkin lanterns were placed on porches and on windowsills, instead of being carried around by children.

## The Origin of Jack-o'-Lantern

When the term Jack-o'-Lantern first appeared in 1750, it referred to a night watchman or a man employed to carry a lantern. It is likely that this nickname was derived from the well-known Halloween story of Jack and the devil.

The original Jack was said to be a roguish but crafty Irish blacksmith. On the night that Jack was due to die, the devil appeared to collect his soul. Using all his cunning, the blacksmith managed to trick the devil into transforming himself into a sixpence in order to pay for one last drink on earth. Instead of paying for the drink, Jack stuffed the devil into his purse, in which he had placed a silver cross. The power of the cross stopped the devil from changing back to his original form

and he was trapped. Jack refused to let the devil out of his purse unless the devil left Jack for another ten years on earth.

When the ten years were up, the devil returned to claim him, but Jack managed to trick him again. He persuaded the devil to climb a tree and then carved the sign of the cross on the trunk beneath him. The devil was trapped once more. This time, Jack insisted he would not free him unless the Devil promised never to take his soul to hell.

When Jack finally died, after many years of riotous living, he was denied entry into heaven. He was told to ask for entrance at the gates of hell, but of course the devil would not take him either. The devil cursed Jack, telling him to be gone, and threw a live coal from the fires of hell after him as he went.

In order to light his way, Jack put the ember into the hollowed-out turnip he was eating. His fate was then to wander between the realms of the living and the dead forever, carrying his turnip lantern. The solitary figure of the night watchman making his way through the dark with a single lantern brought the story of Jack to mind, and the name stuck.

BELOW *The fires of hell provided the ember to light Jack's lantern.*

CRAFTS

## Turnip Lanterns

Choose a large rutabaga (known as turnips or "neeps" in Scotland). Slice off any leaves, then cut off the top and hollow out the center. This is fairly hard work and takes a while. Carve two frowning eyes and a growling mouth to make a face.

Make a small hole on either side of the top of the rutabaga—most easily done with a metal skewer. Feed string through the holes and tie to form a carrying handle. Make sure the handle is long enough, otherwise your fingers might get too hot over the candle flame. Place a tea light in the bottom of the rutabaga and carry the lantern with you when you go trick-or-treating with friends.

Until the middle of the twentieth century, Scottish children would eat slivers of raw turnip as a sweetmeat while they were carving their lanterns.

(Always supervise children as they carve and accompany them when trick-or-treating.)

87

CRAFTS

# Pumpkin Lanterns

TO MAKE A PUMKIN LANTERN
YOU WILL NEED:

A serrated knife

A large spoon or metal scoop

A carving saw (essential for detailed
designs, available from craft stores)

A transfer tool (for marking out your
design; you could use a skewer)

Stencils

### Choosing the Perfect Pumpkin

The ideal pumpkin should be large enough to carry the design you want to carve. It should feel heavy for its size when you pick it up. (Pumpkins that feel lighter than they look may have dried out slightly.) Try to get the most unripe pumpkin you can find. This means you can carve your design a day or two in advance and your pumpkin will still be fresh for Halloween. If you are lucky enough to cut your own pumpkin, leave at least a 3-inch (7.5-cm) stem and this will keep your pumpkin fresh longer.

### Creating Your Design

First of all, consider your design. If this is your first attempt at pumpkin-carving, it makes sense to choose a relatively easy pattern. Try looking through children's books for designs to copy. Scowling faces, bats, and evil-looking eyes with a sinister smile make good beginners' choices.

Draw (or copy) your design onto a piece of paper that is large enough to cover the side of your pumpkin. Make it very clear which pieces of the design are to be cut out (color these black) and which pieces are to remain (leave these white).

ABOVE *A stencil enables you to carve out a ghost or similar figure.*

### Preparing the Pumpkin

Cut a large hole in the top of the pumpkin to make a lid. It is a lot easier to cut a straight-sided lid (pentagon- or hexagon-shaped) than to try to make a perfect circle. Once the lid is back on the pumpkin its shape is irrelevant, so cut the easy way. Hold the pumpkin steady and cut with care.

Cut a long V-shaped notch in the top of the lid with a sharp knife. This is an essential safety feature, which will let the hot air out of your lantern and stop it from catching on fire.

1 Using a sharp, serrated knife, carefully cut a large hole in the top of the pumpkin, to make a lid.

2 Cut a V-shaped notch in the top of the lid. This will allow the hot air to escape from the lantern and also prevent it from catching fire.

3 Discard the pith and scoop out all the pumpkin flesh into a bowl. Remember that the more you scoop out, the brighter your lantern will glow.

### "Scrape Out" Designs

If you want to create really intricate designs for your pumpkins, the technique of scraping out lets you include much more detail. Scraping out means you don't have to cut the design right through the skin and flesh of the pumpkin. Instead, you simply cut away the top layer of skin, revealing the pale flesh underneath. You can use the same stencil/transfer technique to trace your design onto the pumpkin, but you can choose much more elaborate designs.

BELOW *Scraping out enables you to carve out more detailed, sophisticated designs.*

Remember that when you hollow out your pumpkin, you will need to be more thorough on the side that is to carry the scraped-out design. You don't have to hollow all of the flesh out this carefully, just the part behind the design. If you make sure that the flesh is only about ½ inch (1 cm) thick under the scrape out, the candlelight will be able to shine through and illuminate your design.

When you hollow out the pumpkin, keep any seeds, which can be dried and then planted. Throw away the stringy pith and scrape away as much of the flesh as you can be bothered to scoop out. The more flesh you take out, the brighter your lantern will glow.

1 When your pumpkin is cleaned and dry, trim your design stencil to fit and then tape firmly in place. Using the transfer tool, follow the pattern on the stencil and make a series of indentations on the surface of the pumpkin (these will appear as dots). You need to press hard enough to go through the paper and make a small hole in the pumpkin skin. Don't rush. The marks you make will be your cutting guidelines. Before you take your stencil away, make sure you have traced over every line. The more complicated your design, the closer together your indentations should be.

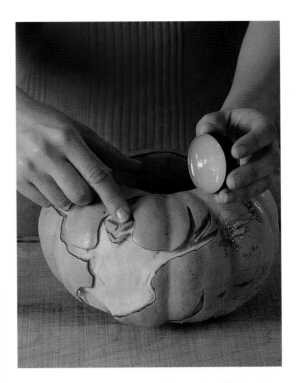

2 Remove your stencil and begin to cut out the pattern. This job is much easier if you use a carving saw. It gives you much better control than a knife and enables you to make precise cuts. Always use a sawing motion and keep the saw at right angles to the pumpkin surface. When you come to a corner, always take out the blade and reposition it. Don't try to saw around the corner, as the shape will not be exact.

3 Remove the unwanted pieces of the design. This is easier if you cut large pieces in halves or quarters. Trim the flesh behind the design at a 45-degree angle. This will give your design a clean straight edge. If you want your pumpkin to last for several days, cover the cut edges with petroleum jelly. This stops the pumpkin from withering. Place a tea light inside your pumpkin.

# SAMHAIN RECIPES: OLD WORLD

## Soul Cakes

*Remember the departed for Holy Mary's sake. And of your charity pray give us a big soul cake!*

In some parts of England, children still go Souling on October 31, a tradition that dates back hundreds of years. Originally, groups went from door to door begging for money for the poor and a soul cake for themselves. For every cake given, they said a prayer for the souls of the dead. As they went from house to house, they shouted:

*Soul! Soul for a soul cake!*
*I pray good miss a soul cake*
*An apple, a pear, a plum or a cherry*
*Any good thing to make us merry*
*One for Peter, Two for Paul*
*Three for him who made us all*
*Up with the kettle and down with the pan, Give us good alms and we'll be gone.*

Money is still collected for the poor, but the prayers are omitted. Soul cakes came in various shapes and sizes, depending on the region in which they were made, and could contain a bewildering variety of ingredients, from ginger and cinnamon to caraway seeds and raisins.

TO MAKE PLAIN SOUL CAKES
YOU WILL NEED:

8 oz/225 g pie crust (or 1 package of already made)
¾ cup/4 oz/115 g dried mixed fruit
(currants, raisins, golden raisins)
1 tbsp dark brown sugar or 2 tbsp honey
1 tbsp sweet butter, melted

### Method

○ Roll out the pastry with a rolling pin and use it to line some nonstick mini-tart pans.
○ Mix the fruit, brown sugar, and butter.
○ Pile a very small spoonful into the center of each pastry shell.
○ Bake in a preheated oven, 375°F (190°C) for 10–15 minutes.

## RECIPES

# Fuarag, or Hidden Charms

Fuarag was originally made in the north of Scotland and was a cooling drink of oatmeal mixed with water. Over time, it evolved into a dish of whipped cream and oatmeal, in which was hidden a ring, a button, a wishbone, and a coin. At Samhain, a large dish of fuarag was made and everyone present ate communally from one large bowl. The finder of the ring would marry and whoever found the coin would become rich. Finding the wishbone meant that hopes for the future would come true, but the button meant poverty.

While Fuarag is rarely eaten in Scotland today, it is still eaten in Eastern Nova Scotia at Halloween. There are numerous recipes for fuarag, but this one includes whiskey, honey, and toasted oats.

## Method

◦ Toast the oats under a broiler for several minutes, or until they are crisp and a pale golden brown. Whip the cream until very stiff and then stir in the honey, Scotch whiskey, and the charms. Place layers of cream and toasted oatmeal in a large glass bowl, hiding the charms in different layers. Place the bowl in the refrigerator for at least an hour. Serve the fuarag by giving everyone a spoon (traditionally wooden) and inviting them to find the treasure.

Do not assemble the Fuarag more than three hours before eating.

TO MAKE FUARAG YOU WILL NEED:

1/3 cup/2 oz/55 g oatmeal

(as fine as you can buy)

1¼ cups/10 fl oz/300 ml cups fresh heavy cream

3 tbsp honey

3 tbsp Scotch whiskey

A coin, a button, a wishbone, and a ring

(The wishbone should be well cleaned and dried and, like the charms, wrapped in waxed paper)

RECIPES

# Barm Brack

Bairin breac, a cross between bread and cake, was traditionally only served on Samhain eve and was used in kitchen fortune-telling. Each cake had a collection of charms baked into it. Whoever found the ring in their slice would marry within the next 12 months or, if already married, would find wedded bliss. The coin symbolized increased wealth over the next year; the bean, contentment. Whoever was unfortunate enough to find the rag or the pea could look forward to a year of poverty or chronic misfortune in love.

## Method

It is traditional to begin this recipe with the ingredients at room temperature. Warm the flour and the sugar in the oven and heat the milk until you can just put your finger in it comfortably. Leave the butter and eggs out of the refrigerator for a while, too.

° Sift the warmed flour, nutmeg, and a pinch of salt together. If using active dry yeast, tip the

TO MAKE BARM BRACK
YOU WILL NEED:

3½ cups/1 lb/450 g all-purpose flour

⅓ cup/2 oz/55 g brown sugar

1¼ cups/10 fl oz/300 ml milk

¼ cup/2 oz/55 g butter

2 eggs beaten, plus 1 egg yolk for the glaze

¼ tsp freshly grated nutmeg

Salt

½ oz fresh yeast (package of active yeast)

1½ cups/8 oz/225 g golden raisins

1½ cups/8 oz/225 g currants

¾ cup/4 oz/115 g candied peel

Strong cold tea: soak the fruit in the cold tea overnight and then strain.

A ring, a coin, a pea, a bean and a piece of rag, each wrapped in waxed paper

sachet onto the flour. If using fresh yeast, blend with a teaspoon of sugar and a little warm milk, then wait for it to froth. Add the remaining sugar to the flour. Add the frothing

## SNAP DRAGON RAISINS

YOU WILL NEED:

2¼ cups/12 oz/350 g seedless raisins

2 tbsp finely sliced preserved ginger

1½ cups/12 fl oz/350 ml brandy
(or whiskey)

Sterilize a clean jam jar. Layer the raisins with the ginger until the jar is full. Pack the raisins down lightly so there is not much air between them. Fill the jar with brandy. Make sure the brandy covers the top layer of raisins. Seal tightly and store in a cool, dark cupboard. You can use them after a couple of weeks, but they will last for 12 months. These are delicious spooned over ice cream and were once used in the game of Snap Dragon (see page 64).

yeast to the milk and add the two beaten eggs. Beat the batter until it is fairly stiff but also slightly springy to the touch. Fold in the fruit and push in the ring, coin, and rag.

◦ Grease an 8-inch (20-cm) cake pan and fill with the batter mix. Cover with a cloth and leave to rise in a warm place for about an hour. Bake in a preheated oven, 400°F (200°C), for approximately 1 hour. Remove from the oven and glaze the top with the remaining egg yolk. Return to the oven for 5 minutes. Cool the barm brack on a wire rack.

◦ Cut the cooled cake into fairly thick slices, trying to ensure the charms are completely hidden in each slice. To avoid any broken teeth, warn your guests that they may find a charm, and check that pieces given to children don't contain any.

PART TWO

RECIPES

# Colcannon

*Calceannann* is famous throughout Ireland as the pre-eminent Samhain dish. There are several time-honored recipes, but all include a ring to predict who will be the first to marry within the next year.

### TO MAKE COLCANNON YOU WILL NEED:

A ring wrapped in waxed paper

1 finely chopped onion or two chopped scallions

¼ cup/2 oz/55 g butter

2 cups/1 lb/450 g pre-cooked, mashed potatoes (kept warm)

A little half-and-half or heavy cream

¾ cup/1 lb/450 g pre-cooked curly kale (kept warm)

1 tbsp chopped fresh parsley

Salt and pepper

## Method

° First, fry the onion with a teaspoon of the butter. Next, mash the potatoes again really well and beat in a little milk or cream until they are very light and fluffy in texture.

° Chop up the kale, then mix it with the rest of the melted butter and stir it into the potatoes. Season the potatoes, then hide the ring at the bottom of the dish. More melted butter and chopped parsley can be added to the colcannon just before serving.

° Any leftovers are traditionally fried until browned and crisp on both sides. Single girls would put the last remaining piece of Colcannon in a stocking and hide it under their pillows in order to dream of their future husbands as they slept.

Colcannon is one of Ireland's best-loved dishes and even has its own song:

Did you ever eat Colcannon
When 'twas made with
thickened cream
And the greens and scallions blended
Like the picture in a dream?

Did you ever scoop a hole on top
To hold the melting cake
Of clover-flavoured butter
That your mother used to make?

Did you ever eat and eat, afraid
You'd let the ring go past,
And some old married sprissman
Would get it at the last?

God be with the happy times
When trouble we had not,
And our mothers made colcannon
In the little three-legged pot.

TRADITIONAL IRISH SONG

## Scots Tablet, or Fudge

Most Scottish households keep supplies of fudge, often homemade, for the guisers who come knocking at the door on Halloween night. This is a foolproof recipe:

TO MAKE SCOTS TABLET
YOU WILL NEED:

4½ cups/2 lb/900 g sugar

1 cup/8 fl oz/225 ml milk

¼ cup/2 oz/55 g butter

⅔ cup/7 oz/200 g sweetened, condensed milk

¼ tsp vanilla extract

### Method

◦ Put the sugar, milk, and butter in to a large, saucepan and stir over a very low heat until the sugar is completely melted. There should be no scratching sound as you stir.

◦ Bring to a boil and add the condensed milk carefully. Keep stirring all the time and cook for about 5 minutes.

◦ Take the pan off the heat and test the fudge. Drop a teaspoonful into a glass of cold water and wait for it to cool, then feel the consistency. If it forms a soft ball, the fudge is ready. If it does not, return the pan to the heat and simmer for an additional 5 minutes: test again. Don't overcook.

◦ When the soft ball stage is reached, take the pan off the heat, then stir in a few drops of vanilla extract and pour the fudge into a shallow buttered pan. While it is still slightly warm, mark it into squares with a knife and leave it to cool.

◦ This produces about 3 lb (1.3 kg) of fudge, which is usually all eaten by the end of the day. Scots Tablet is extremely versatile and you can add different flavorings, including chocolate powder, raisins, or liquor (such as dark rum) to make your own variation.

# Lancashire and Yorkshire Parkin

Parkin was and still is eaten at Halloween and on Bonfire Night. It is a thick, dark cake, scented with ginger. The cake was so popular in the north of England that October 31 became known as Parkin Day.

TO MAKE PARKIN YOU WILL NEED:

⅔ cup/5 oz/140 g butter

⅔ cup /7 oz/200 g light or dark corn syrup

2 cups/1½ lb/675 g molasses

2 cups/9 oz/250 g all-purpose wholewheat flour

1 cup/7 oz/200 g brown sugar

½ cup/4 oz/115 g oatmeal

(not rolled oats)

3 tsp ground ginger

1 tsp baking soda

2–3 tsp vinegar

⅔ cup/5 fl oz/150 ml milk

## Method

° Line a clean, rectangular baking pan with silicone paper. (A clean roasting pan lined with parchment paper could be used.)

° Melt together the butter, syrup, and molasses until warm. Pour this over the dry ingredients. Mix the baking soda with a little vinegar to make it fizz. Pour this onto the dry ingredients. Use the warm milk to lift any remaining syrup from the pan, and pour this onto the other ingredients in the bowl.

° Mix well. This is fairly hard work. The mixture will be heavy and fairly soft. Pour into the prepared baking pan.

° Bake in a preheated oven, 325°F (170°C), for 1 hour. Check the Parkin after about 30 minutes. If it has risen at all, give it a shake to make it sink and return to the oven. When cooked, a skewer will emerge clean from the center of the cake. Cool in the pan then turn it out and leave in a sealed container for at least two days to let the flavors intensify. Parkin tastes great on its own or with butter.

TO MAKE HAR CAKES YOU WILL NEED:

1½ cups / 12 oz / 50 g butter

2¾ cups / 1 lb / 450 g oatmeal

3½ cups / 1 lb / 450 g all-purpose flour

2 cups / 1 lb / 450 g sugar

1 cup / 1 lb / 450 g molasses

½ cup / 2 oz / 55 g candied peel

2 tsp baking soda, 1 tsp salt

1 tsp mixed coriander seeds and fennel seeds

1 tsp ground ginger

RECIPES

# Har Cakes or Thor Cakes

A Yorkshire recipe that may date back to the Vikings, these cakes were originally baked in honor of Thor, Norse God of thunder and lightning. They were traditionally made around the beginning of November. This old recipe makes about 4–5 lb (1.8–2.25 kg) of cookie dough but you can easily halve the quantities. It is interesting to note that the biscuits contain fennel and coriander seeds, both traditionally associated with good luck, long life, and protection, in this life and in the journey to the Underworld.

## Method

° Rub the butter into the dry ingredients. Warm the molasses, then add and mix to a fairly stiff dough. Roll out until the dough is about ¼ inch (½ cm) thick and cut into rounds. Sprinkle with extra seeds and bake in a preheated oven, 350°F (180°C), for 10 minutes.

## PLOT TAFFY, OR TOFFEE

This is an old taffy recipe traditionally made on Bonfire Night in memory of the Gunpowder Plot.

YOU WILL NEED:

3 cups / 1 lb / 450 g brown sugar

½ cup / 4 oz / 115 g butter

¼ cup / 4 oz / 115 g molasses

1 tbsp water, 1 tbsp milk, 1 tbsp vinegar

Bring everything except the vinegar to a boil in a high-sided pan. Simmer gently for 20 minutes, stirring all the time. Test by taking the taffy off the heat and dropping a teaspoonful into a glass of water. If it forms a hard ball, the taffy is ready. Stir in the vinegar and pour into an oiled pan. Allow to cool and then break into pieces.

# HALLOWEEN RECIPES: NEW WORLD

## Pumpkin Pie

### To Make the Pastry

○ Rub the butter into the dry ingredients, then add the beaten egg and milk. As soon as the pastry comes together, stop kneading it. Wrap and allow to chill in the refrigerator for a couple of hours.

○ Butter and line a 9-inch (23-cm) pie pan with the pastry, then cover the bottom with a piece of waxed paper. Fill with dried beans and bake in a preheated oven, 325°F (170°C) for 10 minutes.

TO MAKE PUMPKIN PIE
YOU WILL NEED:

For the pastry:
¾ cup/6 oz/175 g butter
1¾ cups/9 oz/250 g all-purpose flour
1 pinch salt
1 tsp superfine sugar
1 tsp freshly grated nutmeg
1 egg
1 tbsp ice-cold milk

For the filling:
2 eggs
1¼ pint/10 fl oz/ 300 ml heavy cream
1 tbsp maple syrup
2 tbsp melted butter
½ cup/3 oz/85 g brown sugar
1 tsp mixed spices (ground cloves, cinnamon, ginger, and nutmeg)
2½ cups/1 pint/600 ml cooked, puréed pumpkin pulp.
Steam or roast the pumpkin and let any liquid drain away, if necessary. Press liquid out of the pumpkin flesh, then purée. One can of pumpkin is a fine substitute.

### To Make the Filling

○ Beat together the eggs, cream, syrup, butter, sugar, and spices very well, until light and fluffy. (This is much easier to do with an electric beater.) Strain the pumpkin one more time and then stir the purée into the batter.

○ Fill the semibaked pie crust and finish cooking in a preheated oven, 350°F (180°C) for 30–40 minutes, or until the pie is just firm. It will thicken as it cools.

# Cloud Cheesecake

TO MAKE CLOUD CHEESECAKE YOU WILL NEED:

Base:
¼ cup/2 oz/55 g butter
⅔ cup/ 4 oz/115 g graham crackers or gingersnaps
(crushed)
½ cup/2 oz/55 g of mixed chopped walnuts,
pecans, and almonds

Cheesecake mix:
2½ cups/1 lb 4 oz/550 g cream cheese, softened
½ cup/4 oz/115 g superfine sugar
1 tsp pure vanilla extract, 4 large eggs
1 pinch of ground cinnamon
1 pinch freshly grated nutmeg
1½ cups/10 fl oz/300 g puréed pumpkin
(see previous recipe)

## To Make the Base

○ Melt the butter over a gentle heat and stir into the dry ingredients. Press the crumbs firmly into a 9-inch (23-cm) loose-bottomed or springform pan.

## To Make the Cheesecake Mix

○ Beat the cream cheese, sugar, and vanilla together very well (use an electric beater if possible). Add the eggs one at a time and beat until light and fluffy. Reserve one quarter of the cheesecake mix—to this add the spices and pumpkin purée. Beat well. Pour the two cheesecake mixes into the pan in alternating layers, then use a spoon to gently swirl into cloud patterns. Bake in a preheated oven, 350°F (180°C), for 1 hour in the middle of the oven. Test the cheesecake: if still unset, cook for another 10 minutes. Cool the cheesecake in the pan. Ease the edges free with a knife and remove from the pan.

## Taffy Shortbread Tombstones

These are easy to make and are particularly good for Halloween parties. For added impact, you can shake "graveyard dust" over the finished tombstones. The dust is made by adding cinnamon and a tiny amount of unsweetened cocoa to confectioner's sugar and stirring it about until the sugar turns a murky gray.

TO MAKE TAFFY SHORTBREAD
TOMBSTONES, YOU WILL NEED:

For the shortbread:
½ cup/4 oz/115 g butter
½ cup/4 oz/115 g brown sugar
1 cup/5 oz/140 g self-rising flour

For the taffy:
½ cup/4 oz/115 g butter
½ cup/4 oz/115 g superfine sugar
2 tbsp corn syrup
⅔ cup/7 oz/200 g sweetened, condensed milk

Chocolate frosting:
4 oz/115 g good-quality dark chocolate

### Method

○ Cream the butter and sugar until very light and fluffy. Mix in the flour and spread the crumbs out across a flat baking pan (a jelly roll pan is ideal) lined with parchment paper. Bake in a preheated oven, 350°F (180°C) for 20 minutes. Remove the pan from the oven and let the cooked shortbread cool.

○ While the shortbread is cooling, melt the ingredients for the taffy over a gentle heat in a large pan. Cook, stirring, until the taffy lifts away from the sides of the pan. Do not over-heat or the taffy will boil over. Pour over the cooked shortbread and let cool.

○ Melt the chocolate in a bowl over hot water and pour over the cooled taffy. Let the chocolate topping cool again and set.

○ To decorate, cut the shortbread into rough rectangles, and shape the tops into semicircles. Using an icing kit, pipe the names of your guests and R.I.P. onto each tombstone. Serve upright.

## Pan de Muertos, "Bread of the Dead"

Served in every Mexican shop, coffeehouse, and home on the Days of the Dead, Pan de Muertos must either have crossed bones on the top or be shaped like a skull.

### Method

○ Warm the liquid ingredients until they are tepid. Place one third of the flour in a large mixing bowl and add the sugar, salt, yeast, and anise. Pour on the warm liquid and beat until well mixed. Add the beaten eggs and mix again. Add the rest of the flour in small batches until it is all absorbed and makes a soft dough. The dough should be slightly sticky rather than too dry. Knead the dough on a floured counter until it springs back when you prod it; this usually takes 5–10 minutes.

## TO MAKE PAN DE MUERTOS YOU WILL NEED:

For the dough:
½ cup/4 oz/115 g butter, melted
⅔ cup/5 fl oz/150 ml milk
⅔ cup/5 fl oz/150 ml water
3½–5 cups/1½–2 lb/450–675 g all-purpose flour
½ cup/4 oz/115 g sugar
1 tsp salt, 2 packages active dry yeast
1 tbsp powdered anise
4 eggs, beaten

For the glaze:
½ cup/4 oz/115 g sugar
2 tbsp fresh orange juice
2 tbsp grated orange zest

○ Place the dough in a greased bowl and cover with parchment or plastic wrap. Allow to rise for about 1 hour in a warm spot. Punch the dough down gently. Form the dough into skull and bone shapes and leave it to rise again. Bake in a preheated oven, 350°F (180°C), for about 40 minutes. Remove from the oven and set aside while you make the glaze.

○ Put the ingredients for the glaze in a pan and warm over a gentle heat until the sugar has melted. Then bring to a boil and simmer for 2 minutes. Remove from the heat and, using a pastry brush, carefully paint the glaze onto the bread to coat.

○ For an extra-gruesome look, sprinkle while still warm with graveyard dust (see previous recipe). For a sweeter version, substitute fresh orange juice for water.

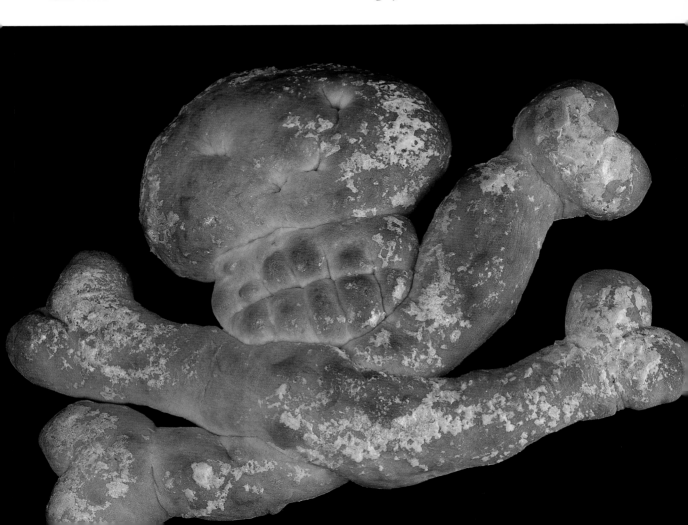

THE FUTURE

# THE POWER OF EARTH, AIR, FIRE, AND WATER

SINCE PREHISTORIC TIMES, *witches and magicians have used "magic circles" to exclude any unwanted influences and to direct the minds of those within the circle away from any distractions toward the magical work they intend to do.*

WHETHER YOU WANT to try your hand at divination, creating good luck charms, or making talismans, you should first establish the right environment for this kind of work.

This simply means casting a circle of protection around yourself so that you have a clear space in which to begin—a space that is set apart from the everyday world. The magic circle acts to keep out those things you do not want (external noises, disruptions, or

ABOVE *Burning incense will cleanse the air and make it fragrant.*

LEFT *Water, salt, incense sticks, and a lit candle for your magic circle.*

distractions) and to enclose those things that you do want (concentration and focus).

Neopagans believe that when you create a circle, you should always invite the Powers of the Elements to be present, so that they can lend their protection and force to the work you do. These Elements are the four natural and magical substances of Earth, Air, Fire, and Water, found everywhere on our planet. In many traditions, Earth corresponds to the compass point north; it is said to govern the senses and to provide protection and wisdom.

Air lies in the east; it governs thought and gives inspiration. Fire is found in the south, where it governs action and bestows energy and passion. Water corresponds to the west; it governs the emotions and grants empathy.

**Method**
○ First follow the path of the sun around your space; walk clockwise, or deosil. Sprinkle, or asperge, the area with salt water as you walk. This purifies and protects the circle.
○ Next, carry the incense around deosil to cleanse and perfume the air.
○ Finally, light the candle and carry it around the circle deosil, bringing illumination and the energizing power of fire to your space. Say:

> I welcome the Guardians
> of the East and of Air
> I welcome the Guardians
> of the South and of Fire
> I welcome the Guardians of the
> West and of Water
> I welcome the Guardians
> of the North and of Earth

Your circle is now in place and you can focus on beginning your work.

When you have finished, thank the elements for their presence and their help; blow out the candle. Walk once more around your circle saying,

> The circle is open, but unbroken.

You can now use your room in a normal way. The next time you wish to create a positive area for divination or for craftwork, just cast the circle again.

# TRADITIONAL DIVINATION

MAN HAS ALWAYS WANTED *to look into the future. The following methods of prediction were all believed to reveal the face or name of a future partner, or to indicate the inquirer's potential prospects for the next twelve months. These traditional, country ways of telling fortunes continued to be practiced every Halloween on the stroke of midnight until the early twentieth century.*

PREDICTION

## The Dumb Bannock

In the northeast of England and Scotland, this nineteenth-century divination was very common among teenage girls, as it was supposed to induce dreams of a potential lover. The girl waited until midnight on the eve of Halloween and then baked a small loaf, or bannock. She did this in complete silence and, having baked the bannock, walked backward to her room. She either ate the bannock or placed it under her pillow and then, still in complete silence, went to bed. Her dreams were supposed to show her the face of the man she would love.

PREDICTION

## The Apple at the Glass

A great favorite with young girls, "the apple at the glass" was believed to reveal the identity of a future sweetheart. If you want to try this form of romantic divination:

⋄ Wait until nearly midnight on Halloween, then carefully peel an apple and cut it into exactly nine pieces.

⋄ Carry these into a dark room containing a mirror, either on the wall or hand-held.

⋄ At the stroke of midnight, begin to eat the pieces of apple while combing your hair.

LEFT *Apple pieces and a mirror: the key to discovering your future love.*

ABOVE *After eating the bannock, girls would dream of a potential lover.*

○ Keep looking into the glass and when you come to the ninth and final piece, throw it over your shoulder.

○ As you look into the glass, the face of your lover should appear.

PREDICTION

## Pulling the Green Kale

This Scottish method of prediction was widely used by farm workers. Like most Halloween activities, it was supposed to indicate romantic prospects for the year. Youngsters would go into the fields at midnight and, their eyes closed, would pull up a stalk of kale. Depending on its shape, the kale stalk, or "custock," would indicate the appearance and personality of a future husband or wife.

If you were lucky enough to pick a large, healthy, sweet-tasting stalk, your future spouse would have a pleasant nature. If, on the other hand, you chose a withered, dried-up stalk,

your future partner would make your life a misery. Those who found earth stuck to the stalk as they pulled it out of the ground considered themselves very lucky; earth, or "yerde," signaled future prosperity.

PREDICTION

## Harrowing the Hemp Seed

On farms all over Scotland, both girls and boys went into the fields at midnight every Halloween and pretended to sow seeds. As they were sowing, they sang:

*Hemp-seed, I sow thee, hemp-seed, I sow thee;*
*And him (her) that is to be my true love,*
*Come after me and harrow thee.*

They then looked over their left shoulders to see the ghostly figure of a prospective partner walking behind them as if working in the field.

PREDICTION

## Pricking the Egg

To hear the name of your future partner:
○ Prick an egg and blow some of the white into a glass of water.
○ At midnight take a sip of this water, but do not swallow it, then walk outside through open fields or woodland.
○ You will hear a voice speak to you and the first name this voice will utter will be that of your future husband or wife.

PREDICTION

## The Pullet's Egg

To discover if you will have good luck in the next 12 months:
○ Separate an egg and drop the white into a glass of water.
○ Swirl it gently with a spoon.
○ If the white sinks right away, then good luck is assured.
○ If it floats or forms strings, illness and bad luck will follow.

PREDICTION

# Reading the Leaves

The art of reading tea leaves originated many centuries ago among the Chinese aristocracy, who believed that their temple bells acted as oracles to foretell the future. Over time, any bell-shaped vessel came to be viewed as oracular, so household teacups became associated with prediction.

"Reading the Leaves" is a favorite form of divination among Romany fortune-tellers, who brew teas from dried hedge flowers and leaves as an alternative to traditional China tea.

Halloween is a perfect night to try the technique of "tasseomancy" for yourself.

## Method

° Choose the cheapest leaf tea you can buy. Cheap tea always has smaller leaf particles,

BELOW *Reading tea leaves is an ancient practice of Chinese origin.*

which makes reading the leaves much easier. Never use tea bags—they are useless for prophecy.

° Make a pot of tea and pour a cup without straining it. Use a teapot with a wide, unfiltered spout so that the leaves can flow easily into your cup. Choose a plain white cup.

ABOVE *Foretell your future by interpreting the leaf shapes.*

◦ While you are drinking the tea, try to clear your mind and concentrate on any questions for which you want an answer.
◦ When there is only a drop left in the cup, turn it swiftly upside-down over the saucer and turn it round three times to the right.
◦ Then tip the cup back up and look at the dregs. They will form a picture of your future.

Traditionally, events that are happening now will appear near the upper rim of the cup.

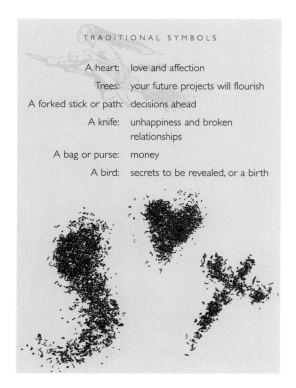

TRADITIONAL SYMBOLS

| | |
|---|---|
| A heart: | love and affection |
| Trees: | your future projects will flourish |
| A forked stick or path: | decisions ahead |
| A knife: | unhappiness and broken relationships |
| A bag or purse: | money |
| A bird: | secrets to be revealed, or a birth |

## THE LEAD AND THE KEY

On Halloween, country people used to risk performing "The Lead and the Key" to predict the future. Lead was melted and then poured through the hole in the end of a key into a barrel of cold water. The lead solidified instantly and the shapes it produced were then interpreted.

Although molten lead is now rightly considered far too dangerous to use, the same effect can be achieved with candle wax. Light a candle, and when there is a large pool of melted wax around the wick, tip it carefully through the eye of a key into a bowl of cold water. It is a good idea to choose a candle that has a contrasting color to your bowl, as this will let you see and interpret the wax shapes more easily.

TRADITIONAL SYMBOLS

| | |
|---|---|
| Ring or circle: | marriage |
| A star or comet: | unexpected news |
| Flower/four-leaved clover: | happiness and good luck |
| Blade or knife: | arguments and unhappiness |

Those in the future will appear in the middle of the cup, and those in the very distant future will appear at the bottom.

PREDICTION
## Reading Coffee Grounds

This is not traditional but works equally well, provided you use finely ground coffee. Greek or Turkish coffee is the best choice, as it is ground to a fine powder. You can make the coffee in a traditional Greek "briki" or in a very small saucepan. Don't let the coffee boil, but keep to a gentle simmer and then pour into a plain coffee cup. Leave it for a minute before you drink it, in order to give the grounds time to settle.

PREDICTION

# Candle Magic

You can try candle magic at any time of the year, but Halloween is a particularly auspicious night for magic that helps us to release and improve our psychic abilities.

## Preparations

Choose a candle. Violet, blue, or purple, all colors traditionally associated with psychic development, are the best choice.

Decide on an essential oil or combination of oils with which to anoint your candle. Lemon balm, mint, camphor, and jasmine are often used to increase intuitive awareness. You can use them individually or create your own blend.

You may feel you want to carve something onto your candle, perhaps an eye, or any other kind of personal symbol that signifies the growth of your intuition (see page 115).

Clear a table and cover it with a black cloth, a candleholder, a bowl with water and

BELOW *Use candle magic to release your inner psychic powers.*

### CANDLE COLORS

| | |
|---|---|
| White/Cream: | Serenity, healing |
| Violet/Mauve/Purple: | Psychic development |
| Blue: | Protection and purification |
| Pale Blue: | Intuition |
| Green: | Vitality, good luck |
| Pale Green: | Serenity, calmness |
| Yellow: | Perception, growth of intellect |
| Orange: | Success, fulfillment, social interactions |
| Red: | Passion, energy |
| Pink: | Love, friendship, happiness |
| Black | Absorbs any negative influences |

salt, a censer of incense, a bowl containing your essential oils, and a carving tool (toothpicks are perfect for candle-carving).

Assemble your tools and your chosen candle. Cast a circle of protection in the usual way (see page 107).

When you have charged your candle, as shown in the steps, it is ready to use. To release the intuitive power of the candle, burn it for an hour a day while the moon is waxing. Use this time for quiet meditation or for practicing your divinatory skills.

1 Sit at your altar and say, "Great powers of the Elements, if it harms none, I wish to enhance my skills of intuition and I dedicate a candle to this aim."

2 Carve your chosen symbol on the purple candle, saying, "As this symbol melts, may my wish be realized and my intuition develop."

3 Anoint the candle with essential oils, saying, "As the scent of these oils is released, may my wish be realized and my intuition develop."

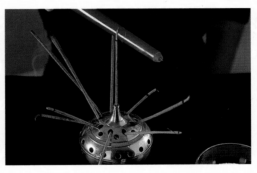

4 Consecrate your candle by passing it through the incense smoke, saying, "I ask for the insight of Air."

5 Next, pass it quickly through the flame of the white altar candle saying, "I ask for the energy of Fire."

6 Sprinkle it with salt water, saying, "I ask for the sensitivity of Water and for the wisdom of Earth. As this candle burns, may my wish be realized and my intuition develop."

113

PREDICTION

## Nut Crack Night

Until the beginning of the last century, it was virtually unthinkable to hold a Halloween party without performing some kind of divination or puzzling one's guests with a collection of Halloween riddles. Country people naturally used whatever was at hand for their predictions and, after the harvest, filberts and chestnuts would have been plentiful. So common was it to try telling one's fortune using nuts that, in the north of England, Halloween was often called Nut Crack Night. Filberts or hazelnuts were placed on the bars of an open fire while the inquirer chanted the following verse:

*If he loves me pop and fly*
*If he hates me, lie and die.*

The nuts were watched carefully. In England, if they cracked, popped loudly, and jumped out of the fire, romantic success was assured. In Scotland, it was hoped that the nuts would jump at the same time; if they did not, the lovers were fated to part in the future. In Sussex, apple seeds were substituted, but the method was the same:

*Pippin, pippin bounce and fly,*
*But if he hates me, lie and die.*

In Scotland, collecting the cob, or filbert, harvest was a big event, which began at the end of September. All local children took part and, in Argyleshire, it was the custom for girls to stitch their aprons in half during the harvest, to create especially large, nut-gathering pockets. On October 31 girls would also bake celebration cakes using filbert flour.

ABOVE *Filberts, roasting on a fire, were used for amorous predictions.*

*Halloween riddles*

*Come a riddle, come a riddle*
*come a rot, tot, tot.*
*There's a little wee man*
*in a bright red coat,*
*A staff in his hand and*
*a stone in his throat,*
*Come a riddle, come a riddle,*
*come a rot, tot, tot.*

(ANSWER: A CHERRY)

*As I was going on my way*
*I saw a tree with apples on it*
*I took no apples from that tree*
*But left no apples on it*

(ANSWER: THERE WERE ONLY TWO APPLES,
SO TAKING *ONE* LEFT ONLY *ONE* APPLE)

# Making a Set of Hazelnut Halloween Oracles

The ancient Celts saw the filbert as the Fruit of Wisdom. Legends told that when the nuts ripened, they dropped into a pool and were eaten by the Great Salmon of Knowledge, who knew "everything that passed over seas, under seas, and in hidden places and desert ways."

Up to the 1950s, Scottish children on the Isle of Skye would gather filberts and drop them into wells and pools to tell their futures.

## Method

⚬ To make a set of Hazelnut Oracles, you need 10 filberts. You can either carve the symbols into the hard outer shell of the nut, or paint them. Witches traditionally use mineral hematite (ground to a fine powder) and oil. This mixture is known by some witches as Earth's Blood and produces blood-red long-lasting color. Scarlet paint is a good alternative and painting the nuts is easier than carving them.

You can make an alternative form of oracle by carving or painting St. Andrew's crosses (originally used as a symbol of truth) onto filberts. Add them to a bag filled with the same number of plain nuts. You can then ask simple Yes/No questions and choose a nut from the bag: X for yes, blank for no.

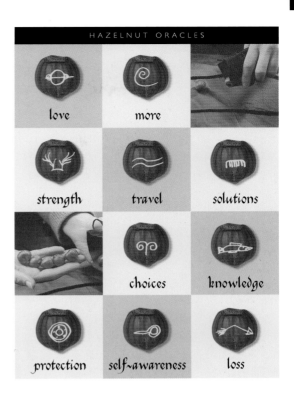

HAZELNUT ORACLES

love · more · strength · travel · solutions · choices · knowledge · protection · self-awareness · loss

ABOVE *These symbols are derived from a Scottish system of divination.*

TELLING YOUR FUTURE WITH YOUR HAZELNUT ORACLE

1 To tell your fortune, place three black cords on a table or on the floor. These will divide your reading into past, present, and future.

2 Place the filberts in a cotton, wool, or silk bag and choose three at random.

3 Throw these onto the table and note where they land.

# SPELLS

*"*DOUBLE, DOUBLE, TOIL *and trouble; Fire burn and cauldron bubble. Fillet of a fenny snake, In the cauldron boil and bake; Eye of newt, and toe of frog, Wool of bat, and tongue of dog, Adder's fork, and blind-worm's sting, Lizard's leg, and howlet's wing— For a charm of pow'rful trouble, Like a hell-broth boil and bubble."*

WILLIAM SHAKESPEARE, *MACBETH*, IV, i

JUST AS WITCHES have always been associated with Halloween, so has the casting of spells. Before the written word was

ABOVE *Snakes are often included in traditional witches' incantations.*

### Early Spell to Exorcise the Evil Eye:

Power of wind I have over it
Power of wrath I have over it
Power of fire I have over it
Power of thunder I have over it
Power of lightning I have over it
Power of storms I have over it
Power of moon I have over it
Power of sun I have over it
Power of stars I have over it
Power of the firmament
I have over it
Power of the Heavens and of the
Worlds I have over it!

*CARMINA GAEDELICA*, VOL II

common, the earliest form of spell-casting (still practiced today in many cultures) was to name a person or object and then to speak aloud your intention. Words were believed to have a power of their own, and the act of voicing your purpose to the universe brought it to life and gave it momentum. To know somebody's true name was to have power over them. In the early Middle Ages, people guarded their own names, the names of their family, and even those of their animals from strangers until trust had been established.

Another significant aspect of spell-casting was to ensure that the spells rhymed and were recited rhythmically. To enchant someone was to do just that, to bring the person under your power by chanting. There are accounts of nine parts; and, in knot-magic, nine knots were tied or untied to effect a magical result.

This old rhyme employs the potency of the number nine and the ancient custom of doubling, which was believed to strengthen the spell. It was used "to rid oneself of a troublesome Adder," (which was a symbol of infertility and corruption).

ABOVE *The moon is frequently invoked in the casting of spells.*

Egyptian, Greek, and Druid priests intoning spells while attendants made music and danced to increase the spell's potency.

It may seem strange to examine ancient spells in a section dealing with the future, but the power and allure of incantation remains ongoing. Spells are created today using the same format as that which was used three or four hundred years ago. The ancient tradition from which they spring forms the basis and the template for the creation of spells used nowadays by modern Wiccans.

## The Power of Three

In many early religions, the number three had profound importance. Ancient gods and goddesses were often depicted with three personalities, a triple face, or three different names, in order to emphasize their association with this magical number. The number nine was believed to be especially magical, as it represented the power of three times three. In most spells, fruit, leaves, or roots were cut into

Underneath his hazelen mot
There's a braggarty worm
with a speckled throat
Now, Nine double has he!
Now from Nine double to Eight double,
From Eight double to Seven double,
From Seven double to Six double,
From Six double to Five double,
From Five double to Four double,
From Four double to Three double,
From Three double to Two double,
From Two double to One double,
Now, No double has he!

RIGHT *Spells were recited rhythmically to increase their magical power.*

117

## Village Witches

As time passed, and pagan habits began to die out, the casting of spells was no longer performed by religious leaders such as priests. However, there were always the wise women and cunning men—village practitioners of magic or healing, who continued to cast spells as and when required.

The spell below was used when sharpening a knife. Using sympathetic magic, the knife's owner named the things that were

> If it were an Aesir shot
> Or if it were an Elfin shot
> Or if it were Witches' shot
> Now will I help thee."

THE SAXONS IN ENGLAND, COCKAYNE

most renowned for their sharpness: a fairy arrow, an elf arrow, and a witch's arrow. As he worked, he tried to enchant a similar sharpness into his own blade.

Eventually, spell craft became the sole preserve of the witch. Magicians existed, but they were usually learned men who concerned themselves with the "conjuring of demons," the study of the esoteric Hebrew doctrines found in the Kabbalah, or with alchemy. Witches were generally country people who relied on traditional knowledge and simple herbalism to achieve their magical ends.

### Evil Spells

Not all spells were benign. The one on the right was used by Isobel Gowdie to prolong an illness suffered by the local Christian minister, Harry Forbes, in 1660. Gowdie described how she mixed together the flesh, intestines, and

> This spell, for curing a fever,
> was recorded in 1662:
>
> For the Feaveris we say thrice over:
> I forbid the qwaking-feavers, the land-feavers,
> And all the feaveris that ever God ordained,
> Owt of the head, owt of the heart, Owt of the bak, owt of the sydes,
> Owt of the kneyis, owt of the thieghes,
> Fra the pointis of the fingeris, to the nebes of the toes,
> Owt shall the feaveris go.
> Som to the hill, som to the hap
> Som to the stone and som to the stok
> In St. Peiteris nam, St. Paul's nam, and all the saints of Hevin,
> In the name of The Father,
> The Sonne and of The Halle Gost!

ISOBEL GOWDIE, 1662

*He is lying in his bed,*
*... is lying sick and sair,*
*Let him lie intill his bed for two*
*monthis and three days mair.*

gall of a toad. To these were added toe and fingernail clippings (she does not state whether they were Forbes'), the liver of a hare, and several rags. These ingredients were chopped up finely and left to soak overnight in water. Gowdie describes chanting the spell while the ingredients were being mixed together.

Once it was completed and magically charged, Gowdie persuaded one of Forbes' friends to smear the potion onto the minister's skin while he lay in bed. There is no record of the efficacy of this spell but Gowdie seemed convinced of its power to do harm to its intended victim.

---

**A HALLOWEEN LOVE SPELL**

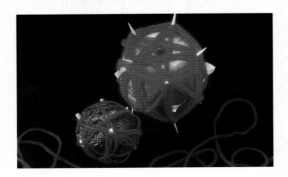

SPELL

## Apple Love Charms

This modern spell is said to help keep both partners in a loving relationship happy, sweet-natured, and at peace with one another:

### Method

**1** Cut an apple in half horizontally to reveal the five-pointed star within.

**2** On a piece of paper, place a drop of your own blood, your name, and the name of your true love or partner. Fold the paper up and place it between the two halves of the apple. Say:

*As the sun moves*
*in the heavens*
*I am yours and you are mine*
*And as the moon moves*
*in her courses*
*You hold my heart*
*and I hold thine.*

**3** Pin the apple back together and bind the pins with red thread to hold the two halves in place. Make the red binding as decorative as possible. Dry the apple and sleep with it under your pillow.

# CHARMS

FOR AS LONG AS THERE *have been spells, there have been magic charms. These are the physical incarnations of the spell's intended effect. Magic charms can take any form, from simple domestic articles such as bags, shoes, or bottles, to detailed figures of clay or wax.*

EACH CULTURE HAS ITS OWN form of charm. In West Africa, juju fetishes are charms that often take the form of small bags containing herbs, seeds, animal teeth, and bird claws or feathers. In the southern United States, practitioners of Vodun (commonly known as Voodoo), make fetish bags called "gris-gris," which contain similar items. Vodun priests are also well-known for their extensive use of Voodoo dolls, or effigies, to effect their various magical aims.

The use of effigy charms is a practice that dates back to Ancient Egypt. Egyptian effigies were made in a variety of substances, including stone, clay, and wood, but the most common form was wax, which could be easily melted and molded into the required shape. These figures were often used by Egyptian priests in order to try to halt the progress of invading armies or to diminish the power of hostile rulers. Spells were carved onto figures representing the enemy and these were then ritually broken, burned, or trampled underfoot.

Similar figures, known as "kolossoi," were created by the Greeks as early as 400 B.C.E. These doll-like effigies were made of lead, wax, or more frequently, clay. Kolossoi served various purposes. They could be used in healing or in the defense of boundaries, but they were most often used for protection. There are numerous examples of kolossoi in Athens, which represent the concept of Victory. They show Victory without wings and thus

LEFT *Shaman woman-chief, by Arlinka Blain.*

120

unable to fly away from the city. Kolossoi have also been found symbolizing Ares, the God of War; these were bound with lead hoops to curtail the God's power and to preserve peace.

In Western Europe, figures known as poppets have long been used by witches for the purposes of healing or cursing. While poppets were used just as often to cure as to cause harm, one of the strongest images still associated with witchcraft is that of the witch plunging a pin into a poppet representing an enemy, in order to haunt or damage him.

The traditional poppet was made of wax or clay and contained physical traces (such as hair or nail clippings) of the recipient of the spell. Some witches strengthened the link between the poppet and its human counterpart by

ABOVE *Voodoo dolls are used for magical aims in the southern United States.*

obtaining articles of clothing or personal jewelry in which to wrap the figure. Contemporary witches now use photographs to make their poppets even more lifelike.

When used in healing, the poppet was stroked, comforted, or rocked like a baby while a spell was recited to drive the illness away. Poppets have also traditionally been used to "bind" individuals, in order to prevent them from harming someone else. In these instances, the poppet fulfilled a similar role to the Greek kolossoi and was pinned, tied, or tightly bound up in order to diminish the power of the malefactor.

121

CHARMS

# Witch Bottles

Early homeowners went to great lengths to protect themselves from malicious witchcraft, a danger they took particularly seriously on October 31. Most people believed that evil influences could enter their homes only through a doorway or a chimney that was open to the sky. In order to protect themselves, they hollowed out alcoves at the back of their chimneys and dug spaces under their front and back doorsteps to house witch bottles. These were usually made of pottery and often contained red wool, urine, and a collection of bent nails, pins, and sharp objects such as broken crockery. The red thread was believed to bring protection while the bent and sharp objects deflected and drove away bad luck. The urine identified the owner of the bottle and the home to be protected.

ABOVE *Witch bottles are traditionally believed to afford protection against bad luck.*

### MAKING A WITCH'S BOTTLE

1 Fill a strong glass or pottery bottle with red thread or wool. Use a knitting needle to help push the wool down to the bottom.

2 Add to it anything you feel appropriate; try coins, beads, bread, salt, beans, or flowers.

3 Seal the bottle and bury it below the doorstep of your home, or as near to the door as possible. Make sure you bury it deeply.

More recently, mason's bottles, containing the names of the master builder, the laborers, and perhaps a coin or ring, were placed under the threshold of a doorway to ensure the safety of a newly completed house.

### Lucky Shoes

Bottles were not the only form of charm employed to ward off potential evil. Both adult and children's shoes have been found hidden in chimneys and roof eaves, apparently put there to bring good luck. There are several theories about why shoes were chosen. Some suggest that as a pair of shoes was worn and repaired for many years, it thus became impregnated with the essence of the owner. Tucking a shoe into the chimney, it was hoped, might fool an evil spirit into thinking it had come upon the shoe's owner: any evil deeds would therefore be directed at the shoe rather than the human. Others think homeowners believed that an evil spirit would be misdirected by the laces on a shoe and somehow become trapped inside it. As recently as 2002 a collection of over one hundred shoes was found in an English house.

Whatever the real reasons for their magical appeal, worn-out shoes remain one of the most commonly found charms. More than 1,000 have been found in chimneys all over Britain.

### CHARMS
## Horseshoes

Horses were revered by early people as creatures of great magical power. By association, both blacksmiths and horseshoes came to be considered lucky and to have the power to drive away evil spirits. It is considered essential to hang a horseshoe the right way up—with the two points at the top and not, as is often seen, facing downward. If it is hung upside down, all the good luck is believed to drain away.

◦ To prevent bad luck from entering and to stop good luck from leaving your house, hang a horseshoe on the inside of your back door.

◦ Add to it a bunch of dried cilantro, tied with a red ribbon, for extra good luck and happiness.

### CHARMS
## Hag Stones

Stones have always been used in magic, and witches value holed stones in particular. Hag stones have a central hole all the way through them and symbolize the womb of the Great Mother Goddess. Witches consider these hag stones to be powerful good luck charms and look for them whenever they are near flint-rich areas.

In Sussex, on the south coast of England, where holed flints are common, hag stones are still hung on strings by the back door to keep evil spirits away.

To increase a woman's fertility:

◦ Find a small hag stone

◦ Wash it three times with seawater

◦ Hang it around the woman's neck on red cord or ribbon like a necklace.

PART THREE

CHARMS

# Making Your Own Amulets and Talismans

Traditionally, amulets were used to protect the wearer from harm and probably derive their name from the Latin "amolior," meaning "I repel." Amulets have always taken many forms, from a simple shell or amber bead, to the Egyptian Eye of Ra or the Hand of Fatima, used in Arabic countries.

The alternative name for amber was originally amuletum, as it was believed to repel ill health and evil. The ancient Celts wore amber for fertility and protection. Today, witches still wear amber necklaces when making magic, in order to deflect unwanted influences. The symbol now known as the Hand of Fatima is found worldwide and the upright hand, palm outward, is thought to deflect evil away from the carrier. This symbol has recently been given a new lease of life in the United States, where the expression "talk to the hand" (accompanied by a turning away of the head and a display of the palm toward the aggressor) is now in everyday use.

## Hand Symbols

In Europe, and particularly in Italy, the symbol of the mano cornuta—first and last fingers extended, two middle fingers and thumb crossed over the palm—is an ancient vestige of the power of the horned god to repel evil. Similarly, the mano in fica—thumb thrust through the first and second fingers of a clenched fist—represents the genitalia of the goddess, a powerful force against evil intent.

TALISMANS

Lucky charms or talismans were made to attract beneficial influences. They may derive their name from the Latin "carmen," or song, which was chanted over the talisman to give it power. To this day, many people choose to carry a

ABOVE *The Hand of Fatima, the mano in fica, and the mano cornuta.*

TO MAKE A PROTECTIVE AMULET YOU WILL NEED:

Amber beads

A small spiral of silver wire—these are easy to make by winding wire tightly around the handle of a wooden spoon and making a small loop at each end. They can also be found in bead shops or magical stores.

Red cotton or leather cord

Beeswax

protective talisman or charm to ensure good luck, and to ward off evil and misfortune.

## Making an Amulet

○ First, cast a circle in the usual way (see page 107). It is better to do this in your kitchen, as you will need to use your oven.

○ Next, warm a small piece of beeswax in the oven, until it is soft and pliable.

○ While the wax is still soft, form it into an evenly shaped bead, flattened on one side.

○ Carve a symbol, such as the palm of a hand, a pair of horns, or an all-seeing eye into the wax.

○ When the wax is absolutely hard, place the bead securely in the spiral and then thread it onto the red cord, between the amber beads.

○ Consecrate your amulet in the usual way

124

(page 107) while asking for the protection of the Elements, Earth, Air, Fire, and Water.

° Recite the following:

*May the powers of Air protect my thoughts*
*May the powers of Fire protect my actions*
*May the powers of Water protect my feelings*
*May the powers of Earth protect my body*

° Thank the elements and close your circle.

**Making a Talisman**

° To make a talisman, follow the same procedure, but instead of carving a symbol to repel evil, choose and carve one that attracts positive and helpful influences.

° Traditional symbols of enlightenment and peace are the Egyptian Ankh (a T-shape with a loop attached to the cross bar), the eight-spoked wheel of the sun, the crescent moon, and the five-pointed star. The five pointed star, or pentagram, has been adopted by modern day Wiccans. The four lower points represent the elements of Earth, Air, Fire, and Water, while the top point symbolizes the spirit which infuses all the other elements.

° When consecrating the talisman say:

*May I be blessed with the inspiration of Air,*
*May I be blessed with the enlightenment of Fire,*
*May I be blessed with the empathy of Water,*
*and may I be blessed with the wisdom of Earth.*

° When you have completed your talisman, you may choose to wear it all the time or for a period from the full moon to the next.

° Good luck talismans have probably been exchanged between friends since the dawn of time.

° When making a gift, you can increase its power by incorporating those symbols or objects that have a personal meaning or relevance for each particular friend.

### MAKING AN AMULET OR A TALISMAN

1 Shape the softened, malleable wax into a bead, flattened on one side.

2 Carve a symbol onto the bead—horns, an eye, or personal symbol of your own.

3 Once the wax is completely hard, insert the bead carefully into the spiral. Thread it onto the red cord, between the amber beads.

# Further Reading

ARKINS, DIANE C., *Halloween: Romantic Art and Customs of Yesteryear,* Pelican, 2000.

BANNATYNE, LESLEY PRATT, *Halloween: An American Holiday, an American History,* Pelican, 1998.

BARTH, EDNA, *Witches, Pumpkins, and Grinning Ghosts: The Story of the Halloween Symbols,* New York, Seabury Press, 1972.

BRADBURY, RAY, *The Halloween Tree,* New York, Alfred A. Knopf, 1972.

BRIGGS, KATHERINE MARY, *The Fairies in Tradition and Literature,* London, Routledge and Kegan Paul, 1967.

DE PULFORD, NICOLA, *The Book of Spells,* Hauppauge, New York, Barron's Educational Series, Inc., 1998.

DONALDSON, TERRY, *The Tarot Spellcaster,* Hauppauge, New York, Barron's Educational Series, Inc., 2001.

GALLAGHER, ANN-MARIE, *Inner Magic: A Guide to Witchcraft,* Hauppauge, New York, Barron's Educational Series, Inc., 2001.

GREEN, MARIAN, *The Book of Spells II,* Hauppauge, New York, Barron's Educational Series, Inc., 2001.

JOHNSON, KENNETH, *Witchcraft and the Shamanic Journey: Pagan Folkways from the Burning Times,* Llewellyn, 1998.

KELLEY, RUTH E., *The Book of Halloween,* Lothrop, Lee & Shepard Co., 1919

KITTEREDGE, GEORGE LYMAN, *Witchcraft in Old and New England,* Cambridge, Massachusetts, Harvard University Press, 1929.

LINTON, RALPH AND ADELIN LINTON, *Halloween Through Twenty Centuries,* New York, Schuman, 1950.

MANTOUX, MARIE-LAURE AND FREDERIQUE CRESTIN-BILLET, *Halloween: Imaginative Holiday Ideas,* Hauppauge, New York, Barron's Educational Series, Inc., 2000.

MARKALE, JEAN AND JON GRAHAM, *The Pagan Mysteries of Halloween: Celebrating the Dark Half of the Year,* Inner Traditions Int'l Ltd., 2001

MELVILLE, FRANCIS, *The Book of Faeries,* Hauppauge, New York, Barron's Educational Series, Inc., 2002.

ORNE, MARTHA RUSSEL, *Hallowe'en: How to Celebrate It,* Fitzgerald Publishing Corp., 1898

SANTINO, JACK, ED., *Halloween and Other Festivals of Death and Life,* Knoxville, University of Tennessee Press, 1994.

SCHAUFFLER, ROBERT HAVEN, *Hallowe'en (Our American Holidays),* Dodd, Mead and Company, 1935.

SUMMERS, LUCY, *The Book of Wicca,* Hauppauge, New York, Barron's Educational Series, Inc., 2001.

WOOD, NICHOLAS, *The Book of the Shaman,* Hauppauge, New York, Barron's Educational Series, Inc., 2001.

## Acknowledgments

Thanks to Vivianne and Chris Crowley for their inspiration and help. To Laura and Nicholas Spicer for their extraordinary kindness, friendship, and encouragement. To Jane Alexander for lots of the most useful kind of advice.

I'd also like to thank everybody who helped with the research for this book, including Robert and Lorraine Henry, Mary Ahmed, Richard Kelsell, Bill Crabtree, and the members of the Northwich Historical Society.

Last, but most important of all, thanks to Robert Chalmers, for everything I take for granted, unfailing generosity, endless help, and always having a laugh.

# INDEX